Sacred Spaces

Transform Any Space into a Sanctuary
for Relaxation, Inspiration, and Rejuvenation

Carolina da Silva

Adams Media
Avon, Massachusetts

Published by
Adams Media, an F+W Publications Company
57 Littlefield Street, Avon, MA 02322. U.S.A.
www.adamsmedia.com

ISBN: 1-59337-019-9

Printed in Canada.

J I H G F E D C B A

Library of Congress Cataloging-in-Publication Data
Silva, Carolina da.
Sacred spaces / Carolina da Silva.
p.   cm.
ISBN 1-59337-019-9
1. Sacred space—Miscellanea. 2. Spiritual life—Miscellanea.
3. Household shrines—Miscellanea. I. Title.
BF1999.S519 2004
203'.5—dc22
2004001160

This publication is designed to provide accurate and authoritative information with regard to
the subject matter covered. It is sold with the understanding that the publisher is not engaged
in rendering legal, accounting, or other professional advice. If legal advice or other expert
assistance is required, the services of a competent professional person should be sought.
　—From a *Declaration of Principles* jointly adopted by a Committee of the American Bar
Association and a Committee of Publishers and Associations

Many of the designations used by manufacturers and sellers to distinguish their
products are claimed as trademarks. Where those designations appear in this book and
Adams Media was aware of a trademark claim, the designations have been printed in
initial capital letters.

Cover illustration by Mark Tocchet.

This book is available at quantity discounts for bulk purchases.
For information, call 1-800-872-5627.

Dedication

To my parents, Verna and Eugene, from whom I learned to appreciate and love home decorating.

And to my friends and colleagues, who graciously gave of their time and ideas in interviews about their sanctuaries, and who helped me fill in the "blank spaces" with wit and wisdom. May your sacred spaces help roll you to glory!

Contents

Contents

Acknowledgments

I'd like to thank the following people for consenting to be interviewed about their sacred spaces. Their responses made valuable contributions to this book. They are: Hyman and Nancy Brown, Thora Chinnery, Poppy Copeland, Shauna Corona, John Dow, Ellen Haynes, Christiane Howard, Ralph Kite, Al Kupczak, Sara Martinelli, Vicki Rubin, Denise Schuck, Barbara Steiner, Diana Vari, Rita Ward, and Hai-Yan Zhang.

Chapter 1

Home Is Where the Heart Is

Do you yearn for a private haven, a retreat from the hustle-bustle of daily life where you can just be yourself? A place of safety and repose, withdrawn from the stresses of work, traffic, chores, and hassles of the outside world, a place where no one can intrude and press their demands upon you? Do you need a sanctuary where you can engage in creative endeavors such as a favorite hobby or writing in a journal? Perhaps you need a dedicated space where you can pursue self-development or spiritual goals as well as meditate, pray, or simply contemplate the universe.

If any of those options sounds appealing, what you're searching for is a sacred space to call your own—though you may not have put it in those terms. "Sacred" in this context doesn't necessarily refer to religion. Instead, the term signifies the sense of a space that is sacrosanct to you. The world isn't lacking for space; it exists all around us, even in our minds. Through the power of our perception and our intentions, we can create that sense of sanctity in almost any space. The way you view your chosen space and the things you do there are the things that matter most.

You may want to consider your entire home a consecrated space, or you may choose to focus on only a corner of it. Your special haven may exist outside your house, too, in your garden, at a park, by the ocean, or deep within a wild wood. If you put your mind to it, you can carve out a little piece of sacred space anywhere—at work, in your car, or even in your hotel room when you're traveling.

BOUNDARIES

When I stop to consider personal space, I can't help but think about boundaries. Boundaries are our personal tools for excluding any unwanted intrusions, but they are also responsible for including all the things you choose to keep close to you. Your choice of surroundings reveals a lot about your individual personality, your preferences, family ties, even your cultural background.

A sacred space is not only a place of retreat. It can be a space to share quiet moments, have fun, or celebrate with those you love. If you envision your sacred space from this perspective, you will see that it can be a place to socialize or to exchange ideas with others. A dining room filled with family and friends is as much a sacred space as an altar or a meditation room. In this way, a boundary becomes a frontier for exploring and interacting with others' personal spaces. You may even discover ways to integrate ideas that you've discovered in other people's homes, offices, or personal retreats into your own space, thus creating a space that is greater than the sum of its parts. This is called synergy.

For as long as I can remember, I've been observing why and how people create and use their private spaces. In my day job I'm an intercultural trainer. There, I've been lucky to get the opportunity to see how people from other cultures design sanctuaries and apply some of their principles to my own havens.

Frankly, I also think I've inherited the home decorator gene. One of my earliest memories involves moving with my parents into a tiny, gray shoebox of a house with all the interior walls painted a depressing shade of army green. The first thing my parents did was repaint the living room a bright yellow. Then they went on to do up the bedrooms in pink and turquoise. In those days, nobody—and I mean nobody—painted rooms in those colors. The fact that everyone considered my parents strange ducks didn't bother them one iota. They enjoyed their bright, cheerful little house that, because of the light, lively paint on the walls, seemed twice as big as any of the other identical boxes on the block.

My dad went on to construct the ultimate private space, a home office that he built over our one-car garage. I call it the "ultimate private space" because you could only get into his office through a secret door that was cleverly hidden inside the bookcase he'd built along the wall inside the attic. Thinking of that attic makes me realize that ever since that time, I've been trying my hand at putting together other sacred spaces. If you're daunted at the prospect of designing your personal retreat, I can definitely tell you not to worry; it's child's play. Here's what I mean.

MY FIRST SACRED SPACE

It never ceases to amaze me that children, unencumbered by adult preoccupations, intuitively know how to do just the right thing. As adults, we could sometimes profit by stepping back into our childhoods to reclaim this knowledge.

I constructed my first sacred space at the age of three without realizing it. On top of a small table in my bedroom, to the sounds of the music from Scheherazade scratching on an old record player, I began to build "Town." This was what I called my miniature village, which I constructed from building blocks, cardboard boxes, scrap lumber, and dollhouse furniture that I either bought or made myself. First, I made little houses of all kinds, fancy and plain, for professional people and the working class. Then I furnished them and peopled them with dollhouse figurines. Over the years, as I spent countless hours "playing," I created increasingly elaborate structures and interiors.

No longer satisfied with simply building and decorating, I had the "residents" interact. They held elections for a mayor and sheriff, disputed amongst themselves, suffered attacks from cowboys, Indians, and medieval knights (or whatever other toy was handy), survived crises, and instigated new hostilities. I now realize that I was working out my own internal conflicts through the townspeople's never-ending soap opera activities. I jealously guarded Town and rarely let my little friends and relatives play with it. I even resented my parents' touching my construction. This was my private place, for me alone!

Town was mobile, too. I could pack it up in boxes when my family moved and set it up in a new location. Eventually Town took over an entire room. In retrospect, I consider Town one of my most therapeutic endeavors, a sacred space that I carried with me throughout childhood and well into adolescence.

ABOUT THIS BOOK

Don't worry! I'm not going to show you how to make dollhouses in this book. Instead, I will offer suggestions on how you can create a haven to bring balance, serenity, and joy into your life. I will discuss ways you can use this space to express your individuality, personal interests, and cultural background. The subjects I cover include ways to design places of intimacy in the home, office, and outdoors, as well as transitory spaces like your car, or a room where you're spending the night away from your home base. I'll also discuss formalized sacred spaces, known as altars. And I promise, you won't need to go to great lengths, or spend a small fortune, to achieve fabulous results.

As a result of having lived around the world, my perspective allows me to supply many examples from other cultures. I also devote a section to creating safe harbors in a foreign environment and offer ideas on how to make a smooth transition to a new home. All along the way you'll find illustrations drawn on anecdotes about sacred spaces I have seen or made myself. I've also interviewed some of my friends and colleagues, who provide a wealth of information on their unique sacred spaces. From time to time, I'll offer a meditation for you to perform in your sanctuary. I even share some delicious recipes to help you relax in your retreat. The appendix contains useful information on colors, fragrances, botanicals, gemstones, totems, and the significance of numbers to help you set up your space.

You don't need a magic wand to transform an average space into a haven. Everything hinges on the stimulation and interplay of your five senses. All you need is to learn a little theory about the five senses, figure out how they relate to your sacred space, and then engage your sense of fun.

So I invite you to grab a sandwich and a cup of coffee and find a quiet corner in that noisy lunchroom at work or the crowded commuter bus, or to clear a space at the kitchen table, and be my companion on a sensual journey of "spacey" exploration.

Chapter 2

Making Sense of the Senses

If you have a hankering for a safe, congenial place to relax, reflect, meditate, and find inner peace, you might want to create some personal space that lets you reach deep into your subconscious. This profoundly influential part of the mind is affected by the stimulation and interplay of the five senses: hearing, touch, taste, smell, and sight.

In this chapter, I'll explain some of the basic principles associated with function of the senses and show what you can do, in a general way, to heighten your perceptions in your sacred space. In later chapters, I'll apply these principles to specific situations.

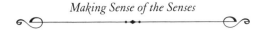

HEARING

I'm sure no one will deny the power of sound—whether it's music, a babbling brook, or a loved one's voice—to pique the intellect and arouse the emotions. Music, in particular, invigorates us by reaching to the inner depths of our beings; it goes places where words don't venture. A beloved aria from a favorite opera can caress your emotions, and a favorite oldie on the car radio can stimulate memories. Music communicates experiences that are richly layered in meaning.

Music can also create a pleasant atmosphere. It helps break the ice at parties or meetings, where people who don't know each other are brought together. Retailers understand the power of music. This is why you hear it playing in the background when you're at the grocery store or shopping mall. Marketers believe that by putting you in a relaxed and happy mood, you will be more willing and open to buying their products. In similar ways, listening to music in your sacred space can make it easier to relax your mind and body, thus making you more receptive to higher states of consciousness.

Music makes an ideal tool for learning because it bypasses the intellect. Think back to all the nursery rhymes and song lyrics you learned effortlessly in childhood (and probably remember today). This is a great example of how music teaches us in a subliminal way.

About ten years ago, researchers at the University of

California Irvine performed a study that seemed to show that college students could raise their test scores if they listened to classical music while they studied. Unfortunately, the public misinterpreted the results, and soon compact discs of classical music for babies began popping up on the market. The thinking was that playing classical music in the nursery would raise kiddie IQs. Nothing could be further from the truth, and "The Mozart Effect," as this phenomenon was labeled, has been largely disregarded.

Knowing this, I still believe that if you're going to use your sanctuary as a space for learning, it can be helpful to have music playing in the background. This is especially true if you like music and don't find it distracting. It doesn't have to be classical. You can choose whatever kind of music moves you—jazz, country, or rock. Simply turn on your CD player, tape deck, or radio and enjoy the sounds of something soothing while you study.

You can also bring harmonious sounds to your home or sacred space through chimes, bells, crystal bowls, or a tabletop waterfall. You may even want to have a simple percussion instrument in your space. Banging on a drum or shaking a tambourine or a pair of maracas can be therapeutic. If you live in a suburban or rural area, consider opening the window to listen to the sounds of nature. At first you might not notice them. But as your mind relaxes, the sounds will make themselves known, and they will soothe you.

SMELL

Compared to animals, we humans are lightweights when it comes to our sniffers. Even so, odor perception remains one of our most acute senses. Memories of our most fundamental life experiences are intimately linked to our sense of smell. I love the scents of autumn, such as the earthy odor of fallen leaves when I crush them underfoot on a walk during a late-season rain, or the smell of chimney smoke curling up into the crisp air as the first fires of the season begin to burn. Spicy-scented apples maturing on the trees, the heady fragrance of warm grapes turning purple in the fields, and the mouth-watering kitchen aromas of hot mulled cider steeped with cinnamon and mace, pumpkin pie, and roasting turkey are all part of the luscious scent memories that that the word "autumn" conjures in my imagination.

Ninety-eight percent of the smells we experience never reach our conscious minds. Instead, the molecules travel directly through the limbic system—the most primitive part of the brain—to the subconscious mind, where the odor affects our emotions. This is why people react strongly, and often irrationally, to smells. One person may dislike the smells of the schoolroom, while for someone else the same odors conjure up the joy of learning. Whereas I may enjoy the ripe fragrances of autumn, these same scents may sadly remind another person of a shattered relationship or of a relative who passed away at that time of year.

Scent evokes primal emotions and helps us tap into a wellspring of vivid images and associations. These recognitions are often more direct, clear, and significant than conscious thoughts. When you incorporate fragrance into your sacred space, you forge a link to this vast part of your mind. This will aid you in self-understanding and self-realization.

Beyond forming a bridge for communication with your subconscious, certain fragrances—such as lavender—can help you rest and instill in you a sense of well-being. This is probably one reason the clean fragrance of lavender flowers has been used for centuries to scent bed linens. Fragrance can also clear your head and infuse your body's tissues with new vitality. Aromatherapists work with essential oils to help cure patients of physical and psychological ills. They claim that fragrance has a restorative effect on the body. Under the right circumstances, fragrance can be so intoxicating that you may be convinced you are inhaling the essence of divinity. There are many ways to add scent to your sanctuary. You can use a perfume diffuser, light-bulb scent rings, potpourris, scent beads, sachets, and the like. You can also burn incense.

On one of my first trips to Great Britain, I was meandering down a cobblestone street in wet and windy Cambridge when I caught a whiff of burning incense. I couldn't tell whether the heady aroma was escaping from an open shop door or the window of a private home. In any case, it had a powerful effect. Immediately, it dissolved my cold discomfort and loneliness at being so far away from my sunny Colorado home. My senses were revitalized, and I was imbued with a deep feeling of well-being. This is the specific power of the scent of incense smoke: it calms and excites, while reaching to the furthest recesses of the psyche to fire the imagination.

Incense was a fundamental spiritual tool of many ancient cultures. The Celtic and Nordic tribes, Egyptians, Greeks, Arabs, and Asians all burned it in religious rites of invocation (in which divine beings were called forth), evocation (to call forth the holy from the worshippers), purification (for people and objects), and offertory (in which the smell of incense was considered an offering to the gods). The Egyptians, on burying their dead, burned special blends of incense to speed the departed souls to their new destinations in the next world. Today incense is used in many religious spaces, including Catholic cathedrals and churches during mass and in Jewish and Buddhist temples as an offertory and devotional.

Some incense blends are characterized as "active." They command, attract, effect change, and drive away negativity. Others are considered passive, and these are burned to establish an atmosphere conducive to spirituality, serenity, and sensuality.

These days, people burn incense in their personal spaces to facilitate meditation, induce a trance state, purify and protect the home, aid in sleep and relaxation, and to stimulate

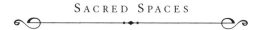
romance. You don't have to make burning incense into a complex procedure, either. Three or four favorite "flavors" of stick incense, which you can find at most drugstores or markets, will probably give you a selection that is adequate for most occasions.

TASTE

As anyone who's ever caught a cold can tell you, taste and smell are almost inseparable. If your nose is stuffed up, you can't taste your food. You've probably heard the old saying, "You are what you eat," a million times. Usually, the speaker hopes to convince his listeners to swallow something to better their health or change their terrible eating habits. I imagine that not too many of us pause to consider the deeper meaning of these words. As we eat and drink, we not only change physically; we also transform our minds and spirits.

Some cultures are so convinced of the mental and spiritual benefits of good food and drink that they can get fanatical about food preparation. The French and the Italians are excellent examples. A former Italian boyfriend of mine, who was also a restaurant owner, once asked me for my recipe for cold asparagus soup. When I told him that I just added a little bit of this and a pinch of that until it tasted right, he refused to believe me and accused me of jealously guarding my "secret" recipe.

Our ancestors knew that food and drink have the capacity to transform our minds and spirits. We have many traditions and rituals that come from this belief. Our practice of toasting the good health, well-being, and prosperous future of a bride and groom is one example.

You can incorporate taste into your haven by using fragrances that remind you of food. For example, you might choose to burn a vanilla-scented candle. Vanilla is a consummate harmonizing fragrance, relaxing you and creating a pleasant environment conducive to social interaction. This is why vanilla incense is often recommended for home blessings. It's also one reason so much sweet comfort food (think cookies, pastries, cakes!) depends on vanilla as a basic ingredient.

Another way to use taste in your sanctuary is to decorate with colors that remind you of food, like apple green, melon yellow, or strawberry red. I chose banana-yellow walls (with a contrasting blue rug) for my office. I love bananas because they taste sweet and energize me, and I like the way the color sets off my framed pictures and memorabilia. I also selected yellow because it's supposed to stimulate the intellect.

I enjoy taking food and drink into my sanctuary. Teas in the winter and smoothies in the summer help me kick back, mull over the day's events, or jump-start my day. I try to use ingredients in my recipes that relate in some way to whatever I am going to do there that day. For example, I drink chamomile tea to unwind, peppermint tea to stimulate me, and kava-kava tea to help produce entertaining dreams.

Diana, a woman in my writers' critique group, also includes taste in her sanctuary by drinking a cup of fragrant herbal tea every time she sits down to write. She told me she hadn't realized it until our interview, but the act of preparing, smelling, and tasting the tea has become a little ritual that she performs to lock her subconscious mind into "writing mode." It also has become a signal to her husband and children to not disturb her.

I've found that drinking something engages all the senses. Appealing refreshments are a joy to all the senses. Listening to the water bubble on the stove alerts my taste buds, and by the time the aroma reaches my nose, I'm usually salivating. Tasting and feeling the textures of different ingredients as they glide over my tongue only enhance the pleasure. In Chapter 6, I've included some recipes for teas and other drinks to enhance your experience in your sacred space.

TOUCH

Think of how boring life would be if you were deprived of your sense of touch. You'd never enjoy the embrace of a loved one. You'd be unable to stroke a pet's fur. You would be completely deprived of contact with the physical world around you. Helen

Keller, who lost her vision and hearing as a baby, was finally reached through her sense of touch. At the moment she realized that touch could communicate words to her, the entire universe opened underneath her fingers.

Fill your sanctuary with a variety of textures, from satin and silk to velvet and Berber wool, with embroidered pillows, cloth wall hangings, and crewelwork throws. You'll have created a feast for your sense of touch as well as for your eyes.

SIGHT

I've saved my favorite sense for last! Shades of light and color are the foundation in my haven, creating a vivid backdrop against which the other senses shimmer and shine. The kinds of light and color I use to decorate my sanctuary help crystallize my sacred space into a harmonious whole so that my enjoyment of it is heightened.

While practically everyone understands that light affects us physically and psychologically, people don't always realize the profound influence that color exerts. To create a harmonious sacred space, you need to know about some of these effects. The therapeutic abilities of color—including its power to soothe and stimulate—have been known, at least intuitively, almost since humankind began keeping records. Color has been used for healing by a collection of cultures from all around the world as diverse as ancient Egyptians, Native Americans, Celts, Asians, Greeks, Persians, and Teutonic peoples.

The art of using color to heal, known as chromotherapy, comes down to us from many ancient cultures. The Egyptians believed that the gift of color healing was conferred on humankind by their god Thoth. They went so far as to construct enormous color halls for healing in their holy cities of Karnak and Thebes. The Greeks healed physical and mental diseases with colored garments and oils. The Arab physician Avicenna, who lived and worked at the beginning of the eleventh century, prepared colored potions made with flowers to cure a variety of ills, from gallbladder attacks to heart disease. Paracelsus, the Renaissance alchemist and father of homeopathy, refined the use of colored waters for healing.

COLOR THEORY

In modern times, a resurgence of interest in the psychological effects of color has prompted investigators to re-evaluate the art of chromotherapy. Nowadays it's a red-hot topic, with plenty of opinions bandied about and much research that still needs to be done. A lot of people have ideas—many of them contradictory—about the effects of different colors in room decorating. Certainty in this area is very difficult to attain. Part of the reason for this is that reactions to color, like reactions to scent, can be very individual. But one thing is for certain: The influence of color on our daily lives is so pervasive it has even invaded our language. We "sing the blues," "see red," "turn green" with envy, work up a "purple passion," immerse ourselves in a "brown study," and laugh at "black humor." Even modern science has felt the need to prove that color is "real" in a tangible sense. Studies have shown that our brains perceive color through the transmission of electromagnetic waves. Color itself appears to have the properties of a basic unit of physical reality, as concrete and individual as a photon or electron.

Advertisers understand how color can influence our opinions, and they take advantage of its magnetism to sell us products. In our contemporary world, we are forever bombarded by infinite shades of every color imaginable in our food, clothing, and environment. Color even surrounds our bodies in the form of a field of energy, called an aura. Though generally invisible to the human eye, auras have been recorded, measured, and even photographed. The color scheme of the aura can tell a good deal about a person's state of health, emotion, mind, and spirit.

In the same way, the color scheme you choose for your sanctuary can reveal a lot about you. Faber Birren, one of the giants in the field of color psychology research, wrote a book entitled *Color Psychology and Color Therapy* that is still widely read by color therapists and psychologists today. Experiments have shown that most people are primarily oriented toward either warm or cold colors. Those attracted to the warm end of the spectrum tend to buy red, orange, pink, and yellow clothes and to fill their environments with these colors. These people are generally open and receptive to outside influences. They are physically active, enjoy social interaction, and openly express their feelings. People oriented toward cold colors tend to surround themselves with shades of green, blue, purple, and black. They are usually more inwardly directed. To others, they may seem unemotional and reserved, and they tend to seek solace in solitary pursuits. Cold-color-oriented people often have trouble adapting to their external environment.

Babies fix their gaze for longer periods of time on bright, richly colored objects, and young children choose color over form when asked to group objects. Small children, when handed black crayons, tend to draw inanimate objects, but when given colored crayons, they draw people, plants, and animals. Since children are attracted to and stimulated by primary colors, it makes sense to decorate their sanctuaries in these shades.

As children, we tend to gravitate toward the following colors, in order of preference: red, blue, green, purple, orange, and yellow. As we age, we tend to favor blue over red, perhaps because our eyes absorb less of the blue end of the spectrum. You may find as you move through different life stages that you want to remodel your sanctuary to fit your changing preferences.

People who dwell in tropical climates seem to prefer red over blue, while those raised in northern climes generally like blue over red. The human eye filters light differently according to how close or far a person lives from the Equator; it has been suggested that this filtering process may account for these choices, which in turn, may affect personal color choices for rooms.

The color psychologist Faber Birren suggests that although color preferences cut across racial lines, gender appears to make a difference. For example, women generally select yellow over orange while men prefer orange to yellow. Popularly, it is claimed that athletes like red, intellectuals are drawn to blue, metaphysicians are attracted to yellow, the convivial enjoy orange, and artists prefer purple.

We all make certain associations with color and food. For instance, red and orange foods (such as apples, cherries, beets, or oranges) are preferred. Yellowish-green food is not appetizing, but the pure green of bell peppers or celery, for example, does have appeal. Yellow and green are also acceptable if they are clear (as in lemonade). Blue, pink, and purple definitely are not considered attractive food colors, unless they're sweets. (Legend tells of a college sorority that—knowingly or not—took advantage of this natural aversion by serving blue-tinted food to all pledges as part of its initiation rites.) On the other hand, shades of orange and brown, such as peach and buff, stimulate the appetite (think pizza and tacos!). Black is not a desirable food color unless you like figs, ripe olives, or caviar. (Yum!)

You can incorporate colors that you associate with your favorite foods into your sanctuary décor to engage the senses of sight, smell, and taste, and thereby triple your pleasure. But here's fair warning: It's easy to go overboard. Let me explain with an example from my own experience. Every time I think of the link between color and food, I'm reminded of a personal failure in home decorating. There is an old carriage house on my property that I rent as an apartment. I decided I was tired of the apartment's stark, white walls. I hired a professional to paint all the walls in a cool shade of mint because the green color seemed to match the "cottagey" feel of the place, which is surrounded by trees, bushes, climbing ivy, and a rose garden. For the molding and the doors, I chose the color complementary to mint green, which is a rich brown shade.

When the painter finished, he stepped back to contemplate his work and commented, "This place sure looks like a hot fudge sundae!" He was right. All that was missing was the cherry on top! The worst thing was that I'd paid good money to have the place ruined. After that, I had a hard time renting the apartment, and tenants didn't stay long. Finally, I caved in and repainted everything in a plain shade of off-white. Live and learn!

Through a condition called synesthesia, some people can enjoy a special, innate affinity to color. You may have experienced synesthesia, at least in brief flashes. Maybe the sound of a certain musical note fills your mouth with the flavor of chocolate. Or maybe, when you feel a cool, misty breeze, you perceive the smell of salt. According to the dictionary, synesthesia is a condition in which one type of stimulation—like a sound or a cool breeze—produces the sensation of another. Some synesthetics are able to perceive colors when they experience certain smells, tastes, alphabet letters, and even sounds. In fact, there are composers who have created entire musical compositions in which sounds are linked to colors.

To some extent, we all possess this faculty. If the idea of fostering a talent for synesthesia appeals to you, you might think of working on developing this gift during meditation sessions. A well-developed sense of synesthesia will add a new dimension to your enjoyment of life.

USING COLOR IN YOUR SACRED SPACE

Here are some suggestions for using color in your sanctuary. A point to bear in mind is that although colors themselves remain fairly constant under changing light, dim light makes color values more vivid, while bright light diminishes them. Colored lights are more dramatic than colored surfaces—your eyes become bedazzled by colored light, but colored surfaces don't affect vision as intensely. This means that you may be more profoundly affected if, for example, you were to shine a green light on your altar rather than placing the altar in a green room. The light filtering through the trees on an outdoor altar produces the most effective atmosphere of all!

If you decide to blend complementary colors into your décor, be aware that blended colors lack the "primitive" qualities of the primary colors (red, yellow, and blue). Hence, they are easier to live with, both at home and in the workplace (unless, of course, you are striving for that "primitive" look). Primary, or pure colors, although initially exciting, do not wear well. In fact, these colors can produce distressing nervous reactions in people who spend long periods of time surrounded by them.

As you can tell from these comments, the effects of color on the human organism are profound, and the associations we make with different colors are complex. To simplify matters, here are some short color synopses for you to refer to as you plan your sacred space.

Red

A hot, dominant, active color, red initially excites the senses. In fact, when measured in red rooms, people's reaction times have been clocked at 12 percent quicker than in rooms of other colors. This color is such an attention-getter that it is used to indicate fire equipment. But despite its initially exciting effect, red seems to have an overall calming effect. If a person spends a good deal of time in a red room, her pulse rate and blood pressure will drop. In this sense, a red room may provide an excellent venue for meditation, especially if you feel drawn to the color. Perhaps this is one reason that many Buddhist temples make liberal use of the color.

However, I don't recommend painting your altar red if it is the portable kind because red colored objects appear bigger and heavier than they really are. A word of warning: red upsets the body's equilibrium, so if you're subject to dizzy spells, you probably should not decorate with it. Red makes a room appear to shrink and is usually not a good choice for a small space. People tend to think they've spent less time in a room where red décor predominates—that's why you see a lot of red décor in bars. The color is said to excite the ego and uplift moods. It's also alleged to initiate action and creativity in the brain but deter execution of projects once begun.

No matter what color predominates in your sanctuary, it's a good idea not to go overboard with any one. A way to create color balance is to include something of an opposite, complementary color in your color scheme. When complementary colors are used together, they produce a sense of completeness. The complementary color for red is green.

Orange

This color exhibits the same warm qualities as red, but many people, especially women, don't prefer it—orange might not be a good color for a fashion designer to use predominantly in a new line of clothing! However, shades and tints of orange, such as peach and salmon, are appropriate for dining rooms because the color is said to stimulate the appetite. Orange is also alleged to foster the intellect. I once painted my bedroom a peachy-salmon color and found it warm and relaxing. An artist friend of mine was so taken by the shade that he painted his living room the same color. He said it showed his paintings to their best advantage. The complementary color for orange is blue.

Yellow

Yellow is the most highly visible color as it is the one the eye focuses on most sharply. Yellow automobiles, for instance, can be seen easily and, all other factors being equal, are the safest color cars on the road. Yellow is a cheerful color that seems brighter than white, and it does not tire the eyes the way white can. Because yellow seems to reduce the size of a room, it is a good color to use when painting large, lofty spaces. It's also a good color choice for a windowless room, such as a bathroom, because the color imitates sunshine. Yellow's complementary color is purple.

Green

Psychologically, an affinity for true green (a mix of equal parts blue and yellow) may indicate a desire to withdraw from external stimuli. Green has been shown to lower blood pressure. This makes the color ideal for concentration and reflection. Green encourages us to contemplate pastoral scenes and other restful thoughts because it does not require the eye to focus. This makes it an excellent color for a bedroom or a meditation space. The spaces where actors await their turns on stage—or on television talk shows—are universally known as "the green room" because green is thought to reduce anxiety and preshow jitters. Green also makes a room look larger. Red is its complementary color.

Many shades of green exist for decorating your sanctuary. For example, yellow-green is a soothing, neutral color. Blue-green has a calming effect that reduces muscular and nervous tension and promotes cardiovascular circulation. The color that is complementary to blue-green is peach (a mix of yellow and orange).

Blue

A favorite color throughout the world, blue is a popular choice for both living spaces and clothing. Blue is a cool, relaxing, and passive color, and its calming effect can help you execute tasks successfully. Test subjects placed in blue rooms tend to feel that they've spent more time there than they actually have. Blue-colored objects appear lighter and smaller. The color also reduces the appetite, so if you'd like to lose weight, you might consider painting your dining room blue. Be aware, however, that blue makes a large room appear even larger and somewhat cold, so it's not necessarily a good choice for big spaces.

Since blue light is difficult to focus on, it's better for rooms designed for rest and relaxation, such as bedrooms, rather than areas where detailed work, reading, or intense study are intended. Orange is blue's complementary color.

Purple

Like blue, purple focuses light softly, so it's not a good color for a room where you spend much of your time reading or doing close work. On the other hand, purple has a universal aesthetic appeal because it combines the earthiness of red with the otherworldly qualities of blue. Purple or violet-colored rooms tend to be tranquilizing. The color complementary to purple is yellow.

White

White is a spiritual, balanced, clear, neutral color. Pure, white sunlight contains all of the seven colors of the visible spectrum. All-white walls are not recommended for your sanctuary because the brightness of white causes the pupil of the eye to close, and it can distract your attention and even cause headaches. The starkness of white walls has been known to drive emotionally disturbed patients into a frenzy. These days, I see so many home interiors painted completely white that I sometimes wonder whether this color scheme is contributing to the tension in contemporary society. If you want to use white in your sanctuary, I suggest you do so sparingly as an accent to your overall color scheme. The opposite of white is black.

B l a c k

Although black is a good shade to use when you want to concentrate in deep meditation, I suggest you stick to black candles and altar cloths instead of painting your entire room this color. A friend of mine once tried to convert her spare bedroom into a meditation space by painting it completely black, including the ceiling and floor. When I went there, I felt depressed and claustrophobic, almost to the point of choking. I lost touch with reality and felt as if I were floating in a fathomless void. Evidently my friend wasn't satisfied either, because she eventually lightened the room with purple, violet, and yellow wallpaper. She also scraped the paint off the floor and stained it brown. Then she added splashes of color, including some white (the opposite of black), magenta, and purple meditation pillows and a table with a vase of white silk calla lilies.

If you're intrigued by black and want to find a productive way to use it, here's a meditation that relies on the "power" of black.

MEDITATION IN BLACK TO DRAW A MIRACLE FROM AN IMPOSSIBLE SITUATION

Take a black candle and rub it with honeysuckle oil. Place it in a candleholder, and set it on top of your dresser, coffee table, or anywhere you can sit for fifteen minutes to meditate undisturbed. Take an incense burner, and position it next to the candle. Light a quick-burning coal in the burner and sprinkle *copal negro,* a fragrant resin imported from Mexico, on the hot coal. Light the candles, and take a seat in front of the table. Meditate for a few minutes on the situation that you've tried so hard to change to no avail. Remember all the steps you took to change things and how they failed. Now, mentally put aside all of those thoughts. If you need to, visualize that the negative thoughts are being carried away with the smoke from the incense and dispelling in the air.

Now, inhale the sweet aroma of the incense. Exhale completely. Then gaze again at the depths of the candle flame. Repeat aloud the following affirmation:

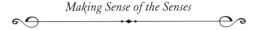

"As life is miraculously created from the void, as the sun, even in its darkest hour, returns to light the earth, may I, too, in my endings find my beginnings. I know that nothing is impossible, and in my state of pure receptivity, the solution to this problem will come to me."

Continue gazing at the candle flame for a few minutes. Don't worry if an answer doesn't come to you immediately, and don't try to force an answer. Just remain open and receptive. After a few minutes, take a deep breath, exhale, and extinguish the candle flame and the incense, if it is still burning. Within the next few days, a solution to your problem may reveal itself to you in a dream or as a thought.

A HOME FOR THE SENSES

Right now you may be wondering how in the world you're going to get the right mix of harmonious sense stimulators in your room. Although it takes some planning and experimentation, it's not as difficult as you might think. Your intuition will do a lot to guide you. Really! Let me give you an example.

A couple of years ago, I volunteered as a guide at one of the homes on our town's historic house tour. The home I worked at was a sweet, little Craftsman-style structure, built to look like an English Tudor, with stone and stucco walls and lots of rich, dark oak paneling. Our house tour takes place during the winter holidays, and the weather is often cold and snowy. That year, however, the sun shone and the temperature rose to toasty sixty degrees.

It seemed that everybody, once they toured the house, wanted to sit on the back patio and take a rest. This was disconcerting for us volunteers, who needed to keep traffic flowing. Every so often, one of us had to step outside and remind people that there were other houses to see on the tour and that if they stayed too long, they might cause a bottleneck. Reluctantly, people eventually moved on.

On my break, I decided to take a good look at the patio to discover what made it so inviting. It was nestled into a corner formed by a couple of rough but warm sandstone walls, softened by creeping, green English ivy. Matching sandstone blocks covered the ground. Five Celtic knots, four small corner ones, and a large central knot bounded by circles, were sandblasted into the stone. This motif fit well with the Craftsman style.

A plaster fountain shaped like a big old toad, painted green and dressed like a butler offering a lily pad instead of a salver, burbled whimsically in a corner. Black wrought-iron tables and chairs were strewn in casual groupings around the patio. The homeowners had set up a five-foot live spruce tree in a planter and placed it on a low stone boundary ledge, decorating it with miniature lights and silver and gold ornaments that glittered in the sunshine. Potted poinsettias amassed on tables, corners, on the ground, and on ledges provided more splashes of color.

I sat staring at the postcard view of the front range of the Rockies to the south. The sun warmed my face as I listened to the fountain and birds chirping in the background and watched the squirrels scamper over damp, earth-fragranced lawn in search of nuts and seeds. I drank in the fresh, tangy fragrance of the evergreens that surrounded me. No wonder the visitors didn't want to leave this haven! This patio stimulated all my senses in such a cheerful but low-key way that even I had a hard time dragging myself back to my post. And I doubt that the homeowners even consciously realized what they had done. They simply combined elements in a way that was pleasing to them.

Now that we've made sense of the senses, let's move on to the next chapters. There, you'll find specific examples of how you can transform various rooms of your house to enliven your sacred space.

Chapter 3

Put a Little Feng Shui in Your Life

You've probably heard of the art of feng shui (pronounced "foong shway"). This Eastern practice has become immensely popular in the West over the last few years as a way to evaluate architecture and interior spaces. In this chapter we discuss how to enhance your personal spaces using this ancient Chinese art.

FENG SHUI: THE ART OF HARMONIOUS LIVING

Feng shui was invented in China 3,000 years ago. It is variously described as the art of placement, the science of good luck management, and a system for establishing harmony in your environment. In short, feng shui is a way to enrich your living and working spaces by attuning them to the laws of nature. Its practitioners believe that applying the principles of feng shui to your immediate environment will help you reap the benefits of a happy, healthy, wealthy life. If arranging your sacred space according to feng shui rules really can help you achieve these goals, it behooves us to take a closer look at the principles and practices of this art.

Feng shui is an outgrowth of Taoism. In this spiritual practice, love of life (*jen*) reigns supreme. The afterlife does not exist, and what matters most is how we live in the "here and now." According to Taoism, everything in the universe is made up of two opposing forces, known as yin and yang. Yin is the earth, water, moonlight, night, death, and rest. It is feminine, cold, soothing, receptive, absorbing, soft, curved, and decreasing. Yang, on the other hand, represents the heavens, fire, sunlight, day, life, and activity. This force is masculine, hot, energizing, giving, hard, straight, and increasing.

Taoism teaches that we should all strive for harmony and balance of the yin and yang forces, as well as an understanding of people's connection to nature. If we can remove the things that impede the harmonious balance of yin and yang in our lives, we can achieve prosperity, happiness, wealth, health, tranquility, and wisdom. Who wouldn't want to do that?

THE ELEMENTS OF MANIFESTATION

In order to help people achieve this yin/yang balance, the Chinese developed the art of feng shui. The art is based on two general principles. The first is that there is a life force, called chí, that flows through objects and nature in general. By practicing feng shui, we can facilitate a positive flow of energy in our surroundings. The second principle states that the interaction of yin/yang forces creates the five basic elements from which all life is created. The five Chinese elements are metal (which corresponds to air in Western philosophy), fire, water, earth, and wood. It is believed that these five elements create order and structure and that they interact with each other in cycle of creation and destruction. For example, the element of fire creates the element of earth but destroys the element of metal.

According to feng shui, you can use representations of the elements in your home to balance yin/yang energies and create a harmonious environment. If you have an overbalance or insufficiency of an element, your environment will be discordant, and you will feel the negative effects. You can remedy the situation by using something made from a harmonizing element as an item of decoration or construction. For example, wood harmonizes the conflict between water and fire, while fire neutralizes the disharmony between wood and earth.

Although feng shui is based on reason, it also relies on the application of intuition to environmental analysis. As you look around, you may intuitively sense an overbalance or a lack of one or two of the elements in a given area of your home. To restore the balance, you might want to remove furnishings or other decorations from the overabundant element and add something from the harmonizing element. You can also include an item in your decorating scheme that is not actually constructed from the element if it is the appropriate color or shape. Consult the following list of the elements and their characteristics for suggestions on how you can apply them to your situation.

ELEMENTS AND THEIR CHARACTERISTICS

Wood

- Effect: Moves the chí upward
- Colors: Blue, green, aqua
- Shapes: Tall and narrow
- Objects: Plants, trees, columns, wooden furniture, vertical stripes, jungle prints, flowers, cotton, rayon, linen fabrics

Fire

- Effect: Moves the chí outward
- Color: Red

- Shapes: Pyramid, triangle, cone
- Objects: Fireplaces, candles, lamps, sunshine, animal products and designs, sunflowers, geometric abstracts

Earth

- Effect: Acts as a pivot in moving chí
- Colors: Earth tones, yellow
- Shapes: Square, rectangle, flat surface
- Objects: Soil (berms, for example), pottery, checked material, bulky furniture

Metal

- Effect: Condenses chí and moves it inward
- Colors: Pastels, white, cream, silver, gold, copper
- Shapes: Oval, round, arch, dome
- Objects: Furniture or jewelry made from metal, gemstones, mobiles, wind chimes, bells, polka-dot material

Water

- Effect: Causes the chí to flow
- Colors: Blue, green, black
- Shapes: Undulating, curved, asymmetrical shapes

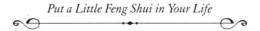

- Objects: Fountains, waterfalls, reflective objects like mirrors or pools, shimmering fabrics, tie-dyes

As you can see, some of the these items are not constructed from the actual element in question. Instead, their shapes, colors, and other characteristics are considered manifestations of the element.

Later in this chapter, when we discuss the nine areas of the home, I will suggest specific uses of the elements. For now, it's time to focus on chí, the other key principle important to feng shui.

CHÍ, THE ESSENCE OF LIFE

Chí is the term used to describe the essential energy of life and its movement. It is believed that when chí flows smoothly in a meandering pattern, it is moving in harmony with the laws of nature. Surrounding yourself with gentle, positive chí will put you in resonance with your environment and draw good luck, wealth, and happiness. When you embrace chí, you are "going with the flow," so to speak.

On the other hand, if you allow the chí in your environment to stagnate, linger, rush by too quickly, or provoke, you disrupt the flow of chí and incur *sha* (literally, "an obnoxious vapor"). This negative energy can incur bad luck and misfortune.

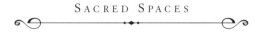
FENG SHUI AND YOUR HOME

Your entire house, from the largest room to the smallest nook and cranny, is considered to be sacred space, where the principles of yin/yang, the elements, and chí can be observed and put into practice. In China, people consult with feng shui masters before building their houses or business establishments to make sure that they can take advantage of the best possible chí.

There are many schools of feng shui, and to become a master of this art takes a lot of determination, practice, and an entire course of study. Some schools use the eight points of the compass as a basis for laying out space: North, South, East, West, Northwest, Northeast, Southeast, and Southwest. Other schools consider the front entrance the most important area of the home, and they divide the sections of the home according to its location.

Feng shui can get complicated very fast. In the modified version presented here, information is combined from both the compass direction and the front door methods. Since we are not considering construction of new buildings in this book, we have to work with the energy flow that is already in your home. This simplified, combination method of feng shui lets you take advantage of various feng shui remedies without feeling overwhelmed. If what I say whets your appetite to learn more about feng shui, I recommend you read more. There are many fine books on the market dedicated exclusively to the subject.

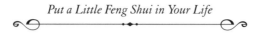

LOCATING THE ENERGY CORNERS OF YOUR HOME

Go to the center of your house, apartment, room, studio, office, or garden. If you live in a house that has more than one story, follow this procedure on every floor. If your home is missing a section, for example, if it is L-shaped, mentally fill in the empty space to make a rectangle. Next, locate the front entrance, and stand facing it. Let's assume that your main door is in the South. This direction is considered the most favorable for a front entrance.

Obviously, we can't all be blessed with South-facing main entrances, so there is a branch of feng shui that assumes your front door and South are in the same location. In essence, your front door becomes your "metaphorical" South direction. If your front door is not really positioned in the South and you are using a "metaphorical South," the descriptions of the eight corners of the home will be valid for both the metaphorical direction you created in your mind and the actual direction on the compass. That is to say, if your front door is actually in the East, the information included under both of the headings "South" and "East" will apply to that area of your home.

WALKING THE NINE LIFE STATIONS

Are you still standing in the center of your home? Good, because I want you to stay there for a moment. First, I will explain how to map out the corners of your home, and then we'll walk to each one together. Imagine that eight straight lines radiate from the center of the space to each of the eight compass directions, like the spokes of a wheel. The ends of these lines represent the eight corners. These are also sometimes called the "life stations" of your home because they represent the major areas of your life, as well as physical compartments. Each corner contains a certain kind of chí energy. If harmonized, this energy flourishes, but if left to fall out of balance, it engenders a particular kind of *sha,* or disharmony and imbalance. Every corner is also associated with certain activities and emotions as well as with an element and a group of colors.

Now I want you to walk from the center of your home to the entrance, located in the metaphorical or actual South. As we have noted, intuition is an important part of feng shui. While you're reading the following descriptions, try to perceive the kind of energy emanating from these areas.

South: Fame and Reputation
The chí flowing from this corner is vigorous and involves the life station of fame, opportunity, respect, reputation, and

dreams. This direction reflects how others see you. The South is associated with the element of fire. The color is red, and the shape is triangular. If the chí flowing from the South gets obstructed, the energy will feel so accelerated that it may leave you exhausted as it rushes by.

In this corner keep framed copies of any awards, degrees, or honors you've received, or articles that have been written about you, because these things will influence what others think of you. To replenish the energy, keep something triangular in this space, like a pyramid or a cone. Candles and aroma diffusers, or lamps with scent rings will also attract vigorous chí to this area. Furniture or decorations made from animal products such as leather, silk, bone, wool, or feathers, as well as fabrics covered with geometric or triangular shapes will also increase the positive energy in this sector. The best place to locate a fireplace or a stove for heating your home is along the South wall. Don't put a water feature in this corner, as fire and water are inimical to each other.

If your front entrance is located here, you might want to decorate it with a colorful, soft-leafed plant to enhance the chí. While all areas of the home should be kept clean and clutter-free, it is of utmost importance to keep the main entrance unobstructed. You want the chí to flow smoothly rather than stagnate or pass by too quickly. It's also essential to maintain the entrance separate from the rest of your home. If you're not lucky enough to live in a home that has a front hall, create one with a screen or a row of plants.

Southwest: Love and Partnership

Move to the right along the first "spoke," and you will enter the love, marriage, and partnership corner of your home. The chí here is soothing and romantic, and the area is associated with purity, peace, happiness, and motherhood. The colors for this corner are pink, red, and white. Avoid the color green and wood furniture. The element is earth, and the shape is flat and square. *Sha* in this area is disruptive and can cause you to behave irrationally.

In this corner keep knickknacks that bring you joy, as well as pictures of loved ones and photos of yourself with other people. There is a belief in feng shui that you should always display knickknacks in pairs—for example, two decorative bowls, two statues, two hearts. If you exhibit a single item or a picture of yourself alone, you may attract vibrations of loneliness and emptiness into your life. While this advice is meant to apply to every corner of the home, it is "doubly" important for the love and marriage corner. Activate this corner by burning a pink candle or by painting the room pink, peach, or white.

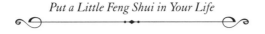

West: Creativity and Children

Move again to your right until you reach the spoke of your imaginary wheel that is located in the West corner of your home. The chí here is calming, making it the ideal corner to enjoy pleasures and indulgences, or to concentrate on children, socializing, and your personal creativity. This is a great spot for your television, DVD player, entertainment center, or even your telephone—especially if gabbing to friends on the phone is a key social outlet for you. The suitable colors for this corner are pastels, cream, and white. The element for this quadrant is metal, while the shapes are ovals, circles, or arches. The *sha* in this corner is dangerous and can cause you to act rashly.

Keep your tools in this corner, your sewing things, small kitchen appliances, artist's easel, computer, or even your journal. Stimulate the energy flow in this area by displaying your favorite gemstones here or by placing a piece of furniture made from metal in this corner. This is a perfect place to hang your children's artwork, too. Be creative and even whimsical when decorating this corner, because creativity is what it is all about. It is recommended that you don't put any red flowers in this corner.

Northwest: Helpful People and Travel

Continue your tour to the Northwest corner of your home. The chí here is expansive. It reflects fresh starts, travel, helpful people, benefactors, interests outside the home, and fatherhood. The element is metal, the colors are black and gray, and the shapes are circles and arches. This area also represents "communications central" for your home, so it is an ideal place for the phone, fax machine, business cards, or an address book. Beware of unpredictable energy emanating from this corner, which can make you feel unsettled.

If you want the energy in this corner to flourish, put a desk here for your computer. Keep materials on the desk relating to new projects and copies of any contracts under negotiation. When activated, this life station can inspire you and promote epiphanies or spiritual insights.

According to the rules of feng shui, all corners are supposed to be well-lit so *sha* is not allowed to accumulate. If the light in this corner is good, start seedlings here to grow. As the little plants grow stronger, so too will you thrive. Don't put any red flowers here, though.

Since this corner relates to travel, why not hang a world map or a poster of a faraway destination you'd like to visit, or decorate with a globe? This is the perfect place to display all those souvenirs from past trips you've collected. As this quadrant is associated with helpful people, you might place a picture of a mentor or a favorite teacher to inspire you. Or perhaps someone you admire has given you a gift that you can display here. If you believe in angels, you might keep a statue or hang a picture of an angel for spiritual guidance. The Northwest is also the "wishing" area of your home, so you can keep in this corner a symbol of a desired wish, such as a picture cut from a magazine of the type of home you'd like to have or a toy cradle to represent the desire to have a child.

North: Career and Life Journey

When you move along the "spoke" to the North, you will be standing directly opposite your main entrance. The chí streaming from this corner is nurturing. It focuses on your career pursuits, life journeys, personal growth, music, and art. The element is water, and the colors are black or any other dark color, such as navy or deep purple. The shape is wavy and curving. *Sha* in this area of the home causes negative influences to linger and can make you feel too lethargic to undertake steps to accomplish your life goals. Activate this corner when you need to get a promotion, close a business deal, or change jobs, or when you're faced with any challenge at work.

Since this corner is associated with water, a good way to increase the chí is to place a tabletop fountain, waterfall, or aquarium here. Make sure the flow of the water is directed toward the inside of the building and not away from it, or all your good luck may flow away with the water! If you don't want to put water in this corner, you can create the illusion of water by placing an object there with a reflective surface, like a mirror, a piece of furniture made from glass, or a crystal. Hang a picture that reminds you of water, like a calm seascape, a painting of a sailboat, seashells, or fish.

You can represent the undulating shape associated with this quadrant with a tapestry, blanket, or upholstery with a wavy print. If you are feeling stuck in your career, cut from a magazine or newspaper a picture of somebody who is very successful in the same field or in the career you would like to pursue.

Northeast: Knowledge and Wisdom

The Northeast corner flows with flourishing chí. This life station addresses knowledge, wisdom, meditation, and spiritual growth. The elemental association is earth; the shapes are low, flat, and square; and the colors are yellow and earth tones. Stagnating chí in this area can make you feel ill.

Place symbols of knowledge in this area, like a bookcase full of books or instruction manuals for all your appliances, or frame and hang an inspirational quotation on the wall. This is another area where you can display a photo of a mentor or favorite teacher or anyone whom you consider to be enlightened. It is one of several good locations for an altar. Appropriate artwork on the wall should reflect tranquil, earthy scenes, such as pictures of mountains or deserts; however, you should avoid plants, especially trees. In this corner of my house, I've placed a miniature figure of a special kind of incense burner that I once wrote about in a novel because the miniature represents knowledge that I have acquired.

East: Family and Health

Chí flowing from the East is stimulating. This corner of the home represents health, family, and rebirth. The element is wood, and the colors are green, aqua, and blue. The shapes are tall, narrow, and cylindrical. This is the space where you can create bonds with family, community, support groups, and religious networks. It is a great place to display objects that relate to your past, like treasures kept from childhood. Or you can exhibit a piece of jewelry or other object that once belonged to an ancestor or member of your family. It's also a good place to store herbs for health or your exercise equipment. Decorate the wall with a picture of a beautiful garden, flowers, or landscapes. Place wood furniture in this corner and decorate with tall, columnar shapes, like a plant on a pedestal, a tall vase, or floral prints. When the chí in this area is obstructed, it can become so overpowering that it makes you feel vain and egotistical.

Southeast: Prosperity and Material Possessions

Complete your tour in the Southeast corner. This area represents wealth, money, and abundance. It is also the place in your home that radiates the most protective energy to guard you from accidents and misfortune. The element for this area is wood; the shapes are cylindrical and columnar; and the colors are red, blue, purple, or even green (as green is the color of money). Never put white flowers in this corner, as they symbolize death.

The next time you visit a Chinese restaurant or store, notice that the cash register is often located in this corner. You may also find a mirror on the opposite wall facing this corner. The Chinese theory about mirrors is that they double the chí of a particular corner. You can take advantage of Southeast energy anywhere in your home. In your office, for instance, you can tape three coins to this corner of your desk. If you are in the field of sales, this is an auspicious place to position your telephone. However, not everything in feng shui is done to create material wealth. For example, if you are performing feng shui for a garden, you might position your sundial in this area to show that you feel your time is more valuable than money.

Activate the Southeast corner by displaying a precious collection of dolls, coins, china, or whatever else you have collected over the years and is valuable to you. Perhaps you own a piece of antique furniture that you would like to display in this corner, or maybe you would like to hang a crystal here to draw positive energy. Remember that placing a mirror in this corner doubles your luck. Just make sure the mirror isn't divided into sections, or your prosperity may get carved up in the same way.

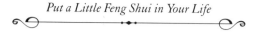

A piggy bank fits well in this corner as a clever way to attract wealth to your life. *Sha* emanating from the Southwest is provoking. It can make you feel irritable and give you headaches.

The Center: Self

The final and most important position of your home is not a corner. It is the place where you began your tour, at the center. This spot represents the self. The element is earth, the colors are yellow and earth tones, and the shape is a square or a rectangle. The chí from all the other corners converge and culminate in this spot, which is why it is the most powerful area of the house. Make sure you keep the center of your space absolutely free from clutter. The center is another fitting place to erect an altar for contemplation and spiritual development.

Since this area is associated with the earth, and is the point where you should feel the most grounded, keep reminders of this element here. Choose items like earthenware vessels or specimens of rocks, minerals, or crystals. Square shapes, like a square or rectangular altar table, fit neatly in this area.

PRACTICING FENG SHUI

Many people don't apply feng shui to their living spaces because they become daunted by all the details. Admittedly, the subject can get complex, given the various schools and myriad points to consider. But as noted at the beginning of this chapter, you can use some feng shui concepts in your home without having to be mindful of everything. Here's another word of advice: Don't feel you need to convert every square inch of your home to conform to the rules all at once, or ever, for that matter. If, for example, you don't like the colors associated with one of the corners, don't feel you need to paint the room entirely in the detested shade. Instead, keep a small object of that color and shape in the area. It will attract just as much positive chí to your environment. Concentrate on changing a few items at a time, or spruce up a single life station that's currently giving you trouble.

SOME REMEDIES

I'm sure you won't be surprised to learn that no space is perfect. It may face a long, straight hall or a street that encourages the chí to rush through too quickly. Your home may be located near a graveyard, or you may have unfriendly neighbors. Your space may be missing one or more quadrants, as in an L-shaped house or room. Exposed rafters may divide a room, or a fireplace may be situated in the most unfavorable Northwest sector, or the toilet may face the door. Never fear! For every feng shui problem, there is a remedy. Here are some ways you can convert harmful *sha* into beneficial chí.

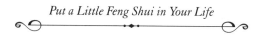
Light

No corner of the home should appear dark or cramped. Add bright lighting to dispel accelerating *sha* and activate positive chí. You can also use a mirror to deflect negativity. Although my home faces the South, for instance, the front door actually faces the West. A full-length built-in mirror has been installed to increase light and deflect dangerous *sha* emanating from that direction.

Color

Use harmonious, pastel shades to calm disruptive *sha,* such as that from the Southwest. Bright colors, on the other hand, will activate stagnating *sha.* If you can't paint an entire room in a balanced color scheme, you can at least add a picture that displays the correct colors.

Sound

Bells, wind chimes, flowing water, and music can all be used to calm provoking *sha.* This is another quality of the *sha* in the Southwest corner, in particular, which makes this a good corner to decorate with these items. It is one of the best corners to install the sound system for your entire home. However, it is also a good idea to use sound in other areas of your home.

Stillness

Calm and quiet can be used as powerful feng shui elements as well. These might include a beautiful decorative object, gemstones, a mask, or even a statue of a smiling Buddha. The goal here is to turn back overpowering *sha*—which tends to come from the East—and create a tranquil ambience.

Movement

In any corner of your home, you want the chí to be as strong and energized as possible, and you want the sha to dissipate. Any decorative element that incorporates motion, especially motion that flows in gentle curves, is a good way to achieve this goal. Incense smoke, wind chimes, waterfalls, fountains, flags that wave in the breeze, mobiles, objects that are decorated with sequins, and even a television will put lingering *sha* into motion and invigorate chí.

Fragrance

Feng shui draws upon the basic principles of harmony and balance, as we have already noted. Paying attention to chí and *sha* is one way to bring more harmony to your space. Fragrance is another. Pleasant smells in the form of fresh flowers, aroma diffusers, incense burners, potpourri, or scented light-bulb rings will draw peace and harmony to the home.

Straight Lines

In feng shui practice, long, straight corridors are usually a no-no. Under some circumstances, however, especially when dangerous *sha* is detected, straight lines can funnel this negative energy away from the house. Use anything that forms a straight line, like the edge of a piece of furniture, a fan, a stick, scroll, flute, or even an oar.

Life

If you feel that the energy in an area is stagnating, add life to it—literally. In terms of decorating elements, life comes in many forms, including an aquarium stocked with live fish, a bird in a cage, or soft, round-leafed plants. Don't use spiky plants, like cacti, because the sharp edges can draw dangerous *sha*.

Devices

Any sort of tool will settle unpredictable *sha,* such as that which comes from the Northwest. Such objects include equipment, like radios or television sets; shop tools, like a saw; a kitchen tool, like a blender; or some kind of electrical apparatus, like a computer. Even a wall calendar or an abacus will do the trick. Heavy objects, like statues and columns will divert *sha* from your environment.

TIPS FOR ENHANCING
THE CHÍ IN YOUR HOME

If you follow its principles strictly, the practice of feng shui can be quite expensive and time-consuming. It can also involve major structural changes to your home. You can definitely enjoy the benefits of feng shui without that level of major commitment. Here are some quick remedies you can employ to create balance and harmonious chí in your environment:

- Keep the toilet seat down and the door to the bathroom closed.
- Cover any drains and fix dripping faucets, or your luck might dribble down the drain.
- Decorate with pairs of knickknacks and lamps.
- Use the color black sparingly, as it is a hue that can drain away chí. One exception is to keep a black rug at the front entrance to attract wealth and luck.
- Throw away dried flowers, as they can create negative energy. You don't need to always use fresh flowers (plastic or silk will work fine), but if you do, discard blossoms as soon as they begin to wilt.
- Remove the clutter from every part of the house, including the inside of the refrigerator, closet, and shelves, and clean these areas thoroughly at the same time.

- Discard faded linens and furniture coverings. Repair anything that is broken, and replace burned out light bulbs immediately.
- If a piece of furniture creates a sharp angle, move it to a spot where it won't disturb the energy flow and where you won't keep running into it.
- Don't place your bed so that your feet face the bedroom door directly. This is known as the coffin position, which obviously is very inauspicious.
- Never put a desk in a position where you will have to sit at it with your back to the door or a window. That way, nobody can stab you in the back.
- Recreate missing corners with mirrors, crystals, living plants, lights, and any of the other remedies.

Finally, once you have arranged your space the way you like it, settle in and enjoy the positive, energizing, relaxing flow of chí as it moves freely around you. You can apply the various principles of feng shui to help you transform every room of your house into your perfect sacred space.

Chapter 4

Altar Talk

"We are swinging high, flying way up, higher than in real life. And when I look down, I see all the ordinary stuff—our brick house, the porch, the tool shed, the back windows, the oil-drum barbecue pit, the clothesline, the chinaberry tree. But they are all lit up from inside so their everyday selves have holy sparks in them, and if people could only see those sparks, they'd go and kneel in front of them and pray and just feel good. Somehow the whole world looks like little altars everywhere."

—Rebecca Wells, *Little Altars Everywhere*

For many people, the word "altar" conjures up a vision of a mammoth dais in the center of an enormous temple. Or perhaps you envision an altar draped in a luminescent cloth embedded with symbols of faith. Maybe religious arti facts, such as intricately carved statues, take a central position. On top of this altar of your imagination, candles send myriad points of light into the hushed darkness of the temple or cathedral. The entire altar, down to the floor, is festooned with vases brimming with flowers. Incense burners carry sweetly fragranced prayers and adorations to the Creator.

Such traditional altars do exist. You can visit the great altars at the Cathedral in Santiago de Compostela, Spain, Westminster Abbey in London, Notre Dame in Paris, and the National Cathedral in Mexico City. Such places act as beacons to draw multitudes of worshippers.

Although, of course, it can be, an altar is not necessarily a place of worship in a religious sense. It doesn't have to be big and ornate; an altar as small as your fingertip can be equally effective. And you don't have to travel to a remote location— you can bring the altar home to you! Home altars have become so popular that providing materials to consumers for their creation has become big business. In some homes, altars have become central locations that serve as repositories of spiritual and sentimental keepsakes, as well as expressions of religious devotion.

Part of what makes a space sacred is the significance of the items there. In our consumer society it is very easy to forget that things have meaning—it's even common for us to pay so little attention that we simply stop seeing things. An altar is a visible, tangible vehicle that you can use as a focal point to concentrate your five senses. What you include on your altar and what to do there is up to you.

Since spaces are made sacred by intent, your motives will define the design and purpose of your altar. You may use it for devotion, meditation, contemplation, or simply as a haven where you can find solitude and "chill out." Your altar may also hold your most important private symbols and mementos that speak directly to your soul as well as emblems of your cultural heritage.

Your altar is a work in progress. It reflects your creative process, which shifts with your changing moods, wants, needs, and mental and spiritual growth. Altars can be permanent or portable. They can also be erected as shrines to honor relationships or one-time events. You can build an altar anywhere—on the fireplace mantle, a shelf in your dining room, the kitchen window, in your garden, on a beach, in a forest clearing, or on a hilltop. My favorite location, and that of many other people, as well, is the bedroom.

YOUR BEDROOM HAVEN

My bedroom is the most logical and natural place for me to commune with the life force and creative energy that flows through the universe. This room represents the central point

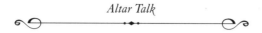

within my safe haven. It's like the hearth that warms my castle.

Have you ever noticed that visitors to your home always hesitate to enter your bedroom? Practically everybody recognizes that nosing around a bedroom is an intrusion, a trespass beyond the boundaries of a private space. In this personal area, you can let your guard down, dress any way you like, and do whatever you want. Since we sleep there, the bedroom represents relaxation, peace, solitude, dreaming, and musing. It's also where many of us retreat to recover from an illness and regain health.

Because a bedroom is such a uniquely personal space, it reflects your life. This reflection includes what's harmonious about it and what's not. So if you want to create a bedroom altar, first off, you've got to take a good look at your room. What do you see? Uh oh! Floor covered with newspapers and clothes? Remnants of meals, empty coffee cups, and books littering the bedside table and dresser? What do you think this says about harmony in your life? The first step toward creating an altar in your bedroom is to get rid of the clutter and give this sacred space a good cleaning.

Once it's clutter-free and neat as a Zen garden, take another critical look at the room. This time, note the kind of lighting, both natural and artificial. What are the window coverings like? Do they block all light when you require darkness, and do they let light filter through when you need that? Or does your room have only one, stark overhead light? Think about what you can do with recessed lighting or lighting that beams upward. At the very least, you can install a dimmer switch on the light or buy a few table lamps and enjoy their cheery, intimate glow.

Perhaps this room could use a coat of paint or wallpaper. You may want to cover the walls in colors that are significant to you and show your room to its best advantage. Next, go for sound, texture, smell, and even taste. For suggestions, go back to the ideas discussed in Chapter 2. Choose whatever elements strike your fancy, as long as they're practical and within your budget.

Fill your room with objects that express your personality. Make the arrangement pleasant but not too busy. Don't confuse the overall sacred space of your bedroom with your altar. The altar is the central point of focus within the sacred space. If your entire bedroom were an altar, your energies would scatter.

YOUR BEDROOM ALTAR

Now that you've arranged the furniture and decorations so the energy flows smoothly and your senses are stimulated, you can concentrate on your focal point. Position your altar anywhere you'd like—near a window, in a corner, on a shelf over your bed,

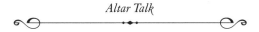
on a dresser, or on a bedside table. If you live in a situation in which a permanent altar in your bedroom is inconvenient, refer to the discussion of portable altars on page 68 for some ideas.

Your altar should balance light and darkness, just as your room does. Many people illuminate their altars with candles. Some follow a tradition that goes back to ancient times and use oil lamps. Still others choose a more modern solution and install track lighting.

Include one or many visually stimulating items on your altar to focus your attention. The subconscious mind responds to symbols better than it does to words, so the objects you choose for your altar should be symbolic of ideas, wishes, or dreams you wish to foster.

Are you using your altar to help you create a significant new beginning or life direction? Then find one key object that is emblematic of that for you. One is a number believed to be auspicious for luck in new endeavors. For example, you might want to place a piece of turquoise on your altar to help manifest your heart's desire, or topaz to keep you motivated to stay on that diet, or an obsidian or other black stone to provide grounding. Refer to the appendix of this book for more information on the traditional meanings of numbers to help you decide how many objects to include.

Don't forget a splash of color, whether it's a symbol made out of cardboard and painted in primary colors or a vase of fresh flowers. You might want to include an incense burner for scent or chimes to catch breezes from an open window. A mixture of pleasing textures, such as a velvet altar cloth, shiny metal candlesticks, or a wool wall hanging as a backdrop can be used to excite your sense of touch. Remember, you are striving to engage all the senses.

Many people include items on bedroom altars that they might not want to put in a more public place—such as a statue of a saint, mythical deity, or even an animal totem. Totems, which are especially important in Native American traditions, are figures of animals that represent different cosmic principles. A figurine of a lion might inspire you to be strong, or a swan could remind you of your internal beauty and grace. A deer might bring a gentle energy to your focal point, while a turtle could represent the bounty of the earth.

Totems have been popular since ancient times when our ancestors gave human personalities and characteristics to the forces they perceived behind natural phenomena. The very antiquity of these personifications helps give them their strength. According to Carl Gustav Jung, the famous psychologist, these traditional forms have become part of the collective unconscious. People's visualizations over time have caused these forms to merge into larger forms, which Jung calls "etheric thought forms," that acquire an existence separate from the humans who created them. This term is just an elaborate way of saying that a totem may possess a power that is bigger than the force that you instill in it. As a result, totems make for very

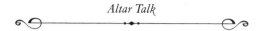

potent symbols for meditation. In case you'd like to adopt a totem, but don't know what to choose, the appendix to this book lists some popular totems along with their meanings.

All that's left for you to do is to find a comfortable, straight-backed chair you can pull up to your altar or some cushy meditation pillows to help you remain comfortable, but alert, when using the altar. Bless your altar in any way you see fit, according to your religious and spiritual beliefs. Some people use salt and water, others use incense and candle flame, and still others anoint their altars with perfume. Do what feels right. Many people associate the incenses frankincense and myrrh with spirituality because they are burned in Catholic churches and in synagogues. Still others reject these scents specifically because they remind them of negative experiences with organized religion. Many associate rose perfume with spiritual topics. They burn rose-scented candles and anoint their altar cloths and candles with the scent. However, I once met a woman who hated roses because they reminded her of the bad relationship she had with her grandmother. Another popular choice, especially for those who are drawn to Asian spiritual traditions, is sandalwood.

Don't feel shy about going to a perfume shop and experimenting with the sample vials until you find what's right for you. If you'd like to use incense or perfume, but don't know what to buy, consult the appendix. It includes short descriptions of the traditional meanings associated with many fragrances.

You may be one of the many people with an aversion to scent. If that's the case, you shouldn't use it at your altar. In the chapters that follow, you will read interviews with different people about their sanctuaries. As you will notice, not everyone has the same ideas about scent.

Do try to use your altar every day, even if you only look at it to relax and feel good. Daily meditation is a great idea, but not everybody has the time or inclination. By acknowledging your altar in some small way each day, you infuse it with a personal energy that will constantly build on itself and become a powerful healing vibration for you. This energy will radiate from your altar and penetrate the furniture, walls, floors, and ceiling of your bedroom to provide you with a safe haven.

A WINDOW TO THE WORLD

Maybe you don't have room, or the funds, to erect a full-blown altar in your bedroom. So why not design a simple window altar? Windows are thresholds that separate the physical plane from worlds beyond, so they're tailor-made to be converted into altars.

As a teenager, I was fortunate to have a big bay window in my bedroom. I packed it with pink and blue pillows, stuffed animals, and a pretty afghan. Every night before going to bed, I sat contemplating the great, tantalizing world beyond the window. A typical teen, I couldn't wait to graduate from high school and strike out on my own. My window faced west, and I took this as a sign that one day, I would, indeed, go west. Two days after graduation, I headed from Detroit to Colorado, where I've made my permanent home ever since.

Even today, the first thing I do in the morning is to get up and look out the bedroom window at the birds and the sky, the trees, and the garden. Gazing out the window puts me in a serene and peaceful mood and never fails to strike me with wonder at the miracle of creation.

It doesn't take much effort to turn your bedroom window into an altar. If you're lucky enough to have a wide sill, you can place candles for meditation, stones, symbolic ceramic figures, totems, and other items there. Tie little bouquets of fragrant herbs or dried flowers from the curtain rod. Hang prisms and crystals in the window, and watch them catch the sunlight and cast rainbows into the bedroom. Look for hanging pieces of stained glass in gift shops. Buy several, and change them with the season or your mood. You can also find pretty, press-on decals with ancient religious symbols that resemble stained glass. If you get some extra cash, or the "spirit" moves you, buy a piece of high-quality stained glass. Have it customized with a personal symbol, and install it in your window.

Something living placed in the window—like creeping ivy or an easy-to-grow houseplant, such as aloe vera, which symbolizes love and bonding—can help forge a bridge between your inner life and the realms beyond. Or you might display a parsley plant, symbolic of victory, and a dill plant, associated with happiness in marriage, in a sunny window and reap the added benefit of fresh herbs for your cooking. Again, consult the appendix for information about fragrances and plants, where you'll also find symbolic meanings of some of the more popular. Meditate at your window altar during different times of day—dawn, noon, sunset, and at night when the moon is climbing in the sky—to experience the effects of different kinds of light on your mind and emotions.

PORTABLE ALTARS

If you can't erect a permanent altar in your bedroom or another preferred space, you can assemble a portable altar. Take all the items you'd want to place on a permanent altar and pack them into a dresser drawer. You can also store them in a box or trunk under the bed or in the closet. Keep extra candles, perfumes, incense, your altar cloth, favorite books on spirituality, and other meaningful objects in the container. When you wish to use your altar, take out the items you want, cover the box with the altar cloth, and set the items on it. An advantage of a portable altar is that it doesn't collect dust the way permanent altars do.

When I lived in Rio de Janeiro, I made a bedroom altar from my steamer trunk. I pushed the empty container against the wall opposite my bed, covered it with a white linen dish-towel, and purchased two inexpensive candleholders and an incense burner. Up against the wall between the candles, I propped one of my books on spirituality that happened to have a full-color glyph on the back cover. The trunk was probably the most "productive" altar I've ever created before or since, in spite of, or perhaps because of, its simplicity.

TRAVELING ALTARS

In our contemporary lives, we spend a lot of time on the go. Although much of what we've discussed so far centers upon ways to still your life and experience peace of mind, I recognize it's not always possible to retreat to a permanent, safe harbor. The times you are on the road in your car, spending the night in a hotel in an unfamiliar city, or even riding the subway are just the times you probably most feel the need to pay a visit to your altar.

The solution is simple. Pack a traveling altar, and carry it with you. Make it small enough to fit inside a makeup case or a shaving kit, or even place it inside your wallet. Model it on the portable altar we've already described, but whittle it down to essential items.

Mexican Wallet Altars

Time for a pop quiz! What did you notice in the last section that seemed a bit strange? That's right, it was the pocket altar. I said that you could carry a portable altar in your wallet. How can you make a traveling altar so small that it fits inside a wallet? Look to Mexico to provide the answer. Mexicans have always been experts at creating crafts in miniature. The wallet altar is an extension of this skill, which depends on assiduous attention to detail.

The craftsperson cuts a piece of plastic into a rectangular shape. Then he cuts another, smaller rectangle, and a third one that ends in a triangle on one side. Next, the plastic is covered on both sides with a brightly colored piece of sturdy cloth, and hand-stitched together with yarn of a complementary color (for example, blue cloth and yellow yarn, or burgundy-colored cloth and orange yarn). The two sides are sewn to the central rectangle to create two flaps. The rectangular flap is folded inward, and the one that ends in a triangle, is folded over it. A snap is sewn in the two ends to keep the altar shut, and voilá! You've got a nifty, basic wallet altar.

When you open up the sides, the altar looks like a triptych with three divisions. Mexicans glue tiny, colorful pictures of saints, angels, Jesus, the Virgin of Guadalupe, sacred hearts, and other religious symbols to the cloth. Any given wallet altar might include anywhere from three to twelve miniature pictures.

Prayers and invocations rendered in miniscule print may also be pasted or stapled to the cloth. Finally, a small medal of a saint is attached to the top edge of the ensemble, directly in the middle. The medal acts as a spine for this little wallet book.

The miniature wallet altar is placed inside the billfold part of an actual wallet or is carried in a pocket or purse. It can be taken out any time to meditate on its message or render a prayer. Think of taking one along on an airplane ride, in your car, or even on your bicycle.

ONE-TIME ALTARS

Remember how the British public turned out and piled floral tributes waist-deep at the Kensington Palace Gate when Princess Di was killed? Enter any teen's room, and chances are very good that you will see a wall plastered with photos and other mementos of a favorite pop star or celebrity. Memorials and shrines like these are examples of one-time altars. You can take this concept and expand on it by building an altar for a specific purpose.

Baby Talk

A friend of mine who wanted to have a baby, but was unable to conceive, went to the local crafts store and purchased a bird's nest made from grapevine and oak moss. She then decorated three eggs like Russian Easter eggs. Eggs are representative of fertility and the female reproductive system, and she chose the number three because it represented her husband, herself, and the baby they wished to conceive. She placed the eggs in the nest, symbolic of the womb in many cultures, along with a piece of turquoise "to make wishes come true," and a prayer folded into a scroll. She tied the scroll with a bright green ribbon to represent fertility. She then placed the nest on her bedroom windowsill to symbolically attract a soul from heaven to the eggs. Every night before she and her husband made love, she contemplated her bird's nest altar for a few minutes. A year later, she had twins!

When she was getting ready to dismantle the altar and return its contents to the ground with a prayer of thanksgiving, she noticed that one of the eggshells had cracked in half, probably on a windy day when the window sash moved and disturbed the nest. She figured that if that eggshell had remained whole, she would have had triplets!

Another friend of mine sadly suffered a miscarriage. During her recovery, she took a walnut shell and glued a tiny, Guatemalan worry doll figure inside. She positioned the shell on a white plate and surrounded it with herbs alleged to absorb pain. Then she placed the plate on her bedside table.

Every time the physical and emotional pain became unbearable, she reached out and touched the plate. When she recovered, she buried the plate along with the herbs and the shell in her backyard and said a prayer to send the soul, who spent such a short time on earth in her womb, back to God. My friend went on to birth two healthy babies.

A Marathon Runner's Altar

I once knew a world-class marathon runner nearing the end of her career who wanted to go out in a blaze of glory by winning at the Olympics. Six months before the date, she began to construct an altar on her fireplace mantle. For the centerpiece, she chose an exquisitely sculpted statue of fleet-footed, winged Mercury of Greco-Roman myth. She fashioned a little crown of dried laurel leaves for victory and crowned the statue. She circled the figure with various medals she'd won throughout her long career. She included newspaper photos, articles, and glossy shots of herself crossing finish lines in victory. She also arranged banners, flags, and affirmations carefully copied in calligraphy. Angels, flowers, candles, several representations of wings cut from satin, silk, and sparkling material completed the tableau along with cards from friends. The finished altar covered the mantle and spilled out over the hearth.

Want to know how the race turned out? I thought you might. This runner wasn't even expected to place. In the last couple of miles of the marathon, she picked up speed, and to the immense surprise of the commentators, steadily passed one runner after another. While she didn't win the race, she did win a medal.

The Wishing Wall

My favorite altar story involves a wall. A friend of mine, a single mom with two small children who all lived together in a cramped apartment, yearned for a house of their own. But Annie's paltry waitress's wages couldn't begin to pay the mortgage on a tent, let alone a house.

One rainy day, she and the kids got together and constructed a collage on the wall of the narrow hall that ran between the bedrooms and the bathroom. They cut out pictures of houses from magazines and books that showed their idea of a dream home. They even tacked up floor plans and glossy photos of showcase gardens, bedrooms, kitchens, baths, and other living spaces.

The centerpiece photo was a big, old farmhouse surrounded by grassy, green fields of ripening corn. In the photo, a little girl played with a dog on the front porch. Pets weren't permitted in Annie's apartment complex, and the boys' fondest desire was to someday own a dog. The family called this makeshift altar their "wishing wall" and often stood before it in rapt contemplation.

Six months passed, and Annie met a recently bereaved widower at a church social. They started dating and found they had lots in common. The man was fond of children, too, and got along well with the boys.

A year later, the couple married, and the family moved into his house. And the house—you guessed it—was almost a dead ringer for the farmhouse in the collage. Only this house was painted a different color and was surrounded by wheat fields instead of cornfields. The groom had bought a puppy to help comfort him over the loss of his wife, and that puppy became the boys' constant companion. When I tease my friend about marrying the man for his house, she just smiles and says, "The house is the kind of place it is because Michael and I share the same tastes."

Occasionally people mention to me that they don't know if they're building their altars properly. In this chapter, I've given you many suggestions about how to turn the most private room in your house into a sanctuary and how to construct an altar, whether it be permanent or mobile. Throughout, I have emphasized that this is a very personal, individualized effort that depends on your wants, needs, and preferences. So if wallet altars are too fussy for your taste, or if, like my husband, you thrive in clutter, or even if you are uncomfortable with formal altars, you don't need to follow up on all of my suggestions. Use the ideas that make sense to you, and fire up your imagination and sense of fun.

Chapter 5

Bathroom Sanctuaries

If you'd asked me when I was a child which was my favorite room in the house, I'd have answered without hesitation: the bathroom. It was my secret retreat where I indulged my secret fantasies. I locked myself in for what seemed like hours—away from family members' prying eyes. In my sanctuary, I pored over letters from boyfriends, cried about lost loves, and planned (but never carried out) revenge against class teases. I wrote my heart out in the diary I squirreled away under the sink behind a big can of Drano. I dreamed my most fanciful dreams in my bathroom refuge. Within its discreet walls, I piled on extravagant amounts of makeup and modeled outlandish clothing combinations my parents would never have allowed me to wear outside the house.

I think that the bathroom is a quiet and private place for many people, a safe haven for contemplation. In this sense, it fits the bill as the quintessential sacred space. Obviously the activity most frequently associated with bathrooms is bathing. So before we discuss how to arrange this sacred space, it's a good idea to "immerse" ourselves in a short discussion of the sacred symbolism surrounding water and bathing.

THE POWER OF WATER

Water is the element that most people associate with bathrooms. Our world and the human body are composed primarily of water. Water is associated with the emotions and the deep mind. This is why in fairy tales and myths there are creatures like undines, mermaids, mermen, kelpies, and other water elemental spirits who are attributed with the power to mesmerize.

From earliest times, our ancestors appreciated and even revered the qualities of water, so they took a good deal of care when they constructed bathing facilities. The oldest known bathroom was built 6,000 years ago in India. In some areas of Iraq, people still use 1,500-year-old toilets and sewer systems. (Do you suppose the plumbing in your house will last as long?)

The art of bathing in ancient times reached its "high-watermark" during the Roman era, when personal hygiene enjoyed a heyday. For example, the baths at Caracalla, built in A.D. 217, held up to 18,000 bathers at a time. So much for a quiet, private time in the bath! Evidently the Romans' idea of a bathing facility was very different from ours. Roman baths almost constituted small towns unto themselves (for example, the town of Bath, England). They often sported gaming rooms, libraries, art galleries, meeting rooms, and temples. A far cry from splashing around in a six-foot tub with a rubber ducky! Romans also installed cold- and hot-water therapy baths and exercise rooms similar to those in our modern health clubs.

Throughout the last couple of centuries, the quality and quantity of our bathrooms has continued to increase. Nowadays it's not unusual to find American homes built with bedroom-size bathrooms complete with gigantic soaking tubs, multihead showers, Jacuzzis, hot tubs, saunas, entertainment centers, and even lounge chairs. I've heard it quipped that when archaeologists from some future century unearth the remains of the United States, our culture will go down in history as famous for our bathrooms. I guess it goes to show that in one way or another, we've all fallen under the mesmerizing spell of those undines and mermaids of ancient lore.

Bathing in Brazil

I gained an appreciation of the power of water and its impact on a sacred space when I went to Brazil on a Fulbright–Hayes fellowship. As in African and Latino traditions like Voodun and Santería, practitioners of Brazilian folk religions immerse themselves in specially prepared baths to purify body and soul. While in the tub, they meditate to open their paths to higher consciousness before engaging in religious rites.

In Rio de Janeiro, I was thrilled to be invited to a private ritual of one of these sects. The priestess informed me that before I could participate, I had to undergo purification. Two gracious handmaidens led me into a tiny bathroom. The tiles on the walls and floor were of the most delicate greenish-blue hue, one that reminded me of the sea. In fact, in a niche high on a wall, a statue of the Brazilian sea goddess, Iemanjá, smiled down on the proceedings. Leafy palm fronds and trailing ivy emerged from the corners of the chamber and crept along the walls. A thousand stars cut from sparkling fabric spread like a protective canopy overhead. I felt as if I'd stepped into a grotto hidden within the mountains encircling the city.

The handmaidens gently removed my clothes and carried them away. They returned with two pitchers containing a mixture of fragrant herbs, oils, and water, and poured the contents over my head, letting the residue drip to the tiled floor and down the drain. I was glad the outdoor temperature was about 100 degrees Fahrenheit, or I might have frozen before I air-dried. As it was, I felt pleasantly refreshed by this herbal purification bath, which the Brazilians call an *amaci*. While they purified me, the women hummed an enchanting song to call on the powers of the Queen of the Sea. The melody reverberated from the walls of the enclosure and combined with the heady fragrance of the oils and herbs to make me feel relaxed but alert and open to new experiences.

Then the women dressed me in the style of the sea goddess, which consisted of a flowing blue robe. They wound a white turban around my head and a lace apron around my midriff, and adorned me with silver jewelry. At last, I was ready to take part in the secret rite . . . which, unfortunately, must remain untold! I can tell you, however, that I will never forget one detail of that intimate, sacred space.

BATHROOM HAVENS

Ready to turn your bathroom into a haven? You can create a permanent sacred space or a transitory one, depending on your requirements and budget. Keep in mind the considerations we covered in Chapter 2 about engaging all the senses. Here is how one woman made a bathroom sanctuary that's also enhanced her creative output as a writer. If you decide you want to design a bathroom sanctuary, perhaps you can derive some inspiration from her creativity. After that, I'll give you some tips of my own.

Barbara's Froggie Bath

My writing mentor Barbara Steiner is the author of more than sixty works, many of them young adult and mystery novels. Obviously she is a very inventive person, whose bathroom sanctuary reflects her creativity along with her love of nature and wry sense of humor.

Barbara claims that her "froggie bathroom" just happened. She started with a fairly small room that had two large, east-facing windows and a turquoise-blue sunken tub. She and her husband built moss rock around the tub and halfway up one of the walls. They bought a matching toilet and two sink basins. They installed the bathroom counter and floor covering to look like grayish-black slate as a reflection of the outdoors.

Barbara explained to me that the rock walls have to be sprayed to keep the moss that is growing on them alive. She doesn't mind performing this chore because the moss makes the tub feel like a pool in the rocks in the woods, which is her favorite place to go to relax and escape the demands of daily life. To further replicate the woodsy feel in her bathroom, Barbara surrounded her tub with plants. A giant philodendron, an enormous umbrella plant, and a few hanging baskets of greenery make a forest-like canopy over the tub. She's also put a cat seat in the window next to the tub. Her cats climb on the perch to snooze in the sun and watch the birds outside the window. Bamboo window coverings can be raised or lowered depending on how much light she wants to let in. Large mirrors cover two walls and reflect more light into the room, giving it a spacious feeling. When Barbara bathes at night, she either turns on the makeup bulbs around the mirror, or she lights several candles that emit a very slight scent.

The frogs appeared on the scene when Barbara realized that this indoor-outdoor environment would make a perfect place for frogs to live. She fell in love with the first Buddha frog she bought—as she told me, they have such wonderful expressions. The collection grew from there, hailing now from around the world. It seems that every culture has frogs and makes art of frogs. Often she purchases the frogs as souvenirs, but friends also give them to her as gifts. Some are made from native stone, such as the one from Italy. The ones from Mexico have cultural scenes painted in miniature on their backs, while her ceramic frogs with their wide-open mouths were made by a potter in Colorado. She's even collected a froggie doubles tennis team as a reflection of her interest in the sport.

Barbara affirmed that she certainly considers the bathroom to be her sanctuary. It is a restful place where she can lie in the tub, soak away troubles, look out the windows to the big trees, and watch the birds and squirrels. The tub is also one of her favorite places to dive into a favorite novel or volume of poetry. She especially likes Thomas Moore's *Care of the Soul,* as she says that the bathroom feeds her soul.

Barbara has also hung a couple of woodsy paintings by a favorite artist on the wall opposite the tub. The perspective of these paintings is such that she can move into them through her imagination. She also keeps a pad of paper and pen nearby, as she has found the meditative aspect of the bath is very conducive to her writing. She's had many an idea for a story or solutions to a problem occur to her in the tub. "Relaxation sends me into my right brain, which is where the good ideas come from," she confides.

Barbara advises readers who want to create a similar sanctuary in the bath to first have a vision of what they want. She suggests thinking about what soothes you and what feeds your soul. Blue and green are colors that make her feel particularly good, but everyone has different feelings about color. Her most important advice is to be aware. If you see a place you like, think about what is there that attracts you, and see if you can incorporate it into your own space.

She also reminds people not to feel they must create the sanctuary all at once. "Start with one object as a focal point, as I did with my tub. Then slowly pick and choose what objects you want to build around it. Sanctuaries are very personal; they need to reflect your individuality."

CREATING YOUR OWN BATHROOM SANCTUARY

As with the bedroom, you'll want to make a bathroom sanctuary that engages all your senses. For the sense of sight, you might want to decorate with symbols of the sea, like seashells, seahorses, mermaids, a fishnet shower curtain, and starfish. Or install a fish tank and fill it with colorful fish. Angelfish are my favorite.

Think of a color scheme that evokes water. Blue, green, violet, purple, silver, and white all make appropriate color choices. For sound, use the stone in the sink described below, play a nature tape with water sounds, or install a sink-top water feature. Many inexpensive and lovely choices are "flooding" the market these days. You can use diaphanous, filmy, or lacy material to cover the window and tub. You can even hang a shimmering, beaded curtain. Do whatever works for you and gives you low, filtered lighting.

Fragrance is important in the bathroom. You can use fragranced soaps, bath salts or oils, body lotions, talc, and colognes. Traditional choices for relaxation include lavender and rose. Vanilla is said to create harmony and balance. Eucalyptus is alleged to ease tired muscles. Some people like to add sensuous fragrances to their bath water. If this thought intrigues you, I suggest you go for the "animal" fragrances, like musk or civet. Add a bit of spice with carnation, allspice, or clove to liven up your blend. You may be the sort of person who enjoys smelling scent in the air, but not on you. In this case, you might try placing a potpourri or a scented candle in the bathroom. If scents bother you, don't feel you have to use them. You can derive benefits from the act of bathing in a pleasant environment without the addition of scent.

Remember to provide yourself with a bath pillow for your head and big fluffy towels, and remember to throw a comfy bath rug on the floor for your tootsies. Comfort and luxury are part of what the element of water is all about.

A Portable Beauty Chest

If you can't drastically modify your bathroom, try bringing in a portable beauty chest. Find a large, pretty container, or make one from a sturdy box and cover it with silvery paper (symbolic of the element water). If you are blessed with an artistic flair, paint symbols of beauty on the box, like flowers, fans, ornate slippers, gloves embellished with pearls and feathers, a mermaid preening herself in a mirror, the Venus symbol, perfume bottles, and whatever else you can think of that is evocative of femininity and beauty. If, like me, you have not inherited the "artsy gene," find pictures in magazines and glue them to the silvery paper along with sequins and glitter.

Inside the box, include a symbol or picture to mount with tape on the wall above the faucet. Don't forget to include a roll of masking tape for this purpose. Put in a couple of small candlesticks, appropriate candles, and a length of muslin or other soft cloth to drape over the counter and/or toilet. Complete your beauty chest with appropriate bath salts, emollients, incense and burner, talc, and a small mirror. Keep it stocked with goodies, and take it along with you when you spend the night away from home. It will provide a comforting touch of home and bolster your self-esteem.

USING THE BATH AS A HEALING SPACE

Now that you've got your sacred space arranged just the way you want it, what do you do with it? For openers, try taking a bath. Do I hear a murmur of protest? Are you telling me that, like so many other people in our hectic contemporary society, you don't have time to luxuriate in the bath? Maybe that's one reason we're a pretty frazzled bunch. Bathing is healing for the body as well as the soul. Baths soothe tired, sore muscles, calm the nerves, and rejuvenate the skin. In fact, the skin is the largest organ of the body, twice the weight of either the liver or brain. Skin protects you from pollution and other injuries, helps you breathe, excretes toxins, regulates your internal temperature, and provides you with strong, sensory stimuli. With all of these benefits going for it, your skin deserves a little extra attention!

You can use Epsom or sea salts to draw toxins from the body and stimulate circulation, while a soothing fragrance such as chamomile will quiet the mind. Meditating in the bath usually gets good results. Many people have difficulty settling down and turning off outside distractions. That's why a bath is a perfect space for meditation. It's quiet, private, and the very act of undressing often moves people to withdraw into their own thoughts. For those of you with the time and inclination, I've developed a bath oil formula to add to your bath water to enhance your meditation sessions. Here's the recipe.

> *Shake together in a 1-ounce bottle:*
> $1/2$ ounce sweet almond oil
> 1 teaspoon Mysore sandalwood oil
> 1 teaspoon rose oil
> $1/2$ teaspoon mandarin oil
> $1/8$ teaspoon French lavender oil

If you don't have a favorite bath fragrance, go to the store and buy one that fits your meditation topic. The fragrance section of this book's appendix will help you coordinate scents with meditation themes. If you can't think of a good theme, then try one associated with water, such as any of these: cleansing, regeneration, creativity, fluidity, receptivity, the female force, intuition, compassion, and divination. Now you don't have to feel guilty about spoiling yourself in the tub because you can make the time productive. In fact, I know a romance writer who claims to do her best creative work while soaking.

Solve a Problem in the
Tub Meditation

Still not convinced that baths are good for spirit as well as the body? I've created this meditation you can perform with or without taking a bath. Simply place two lighted blue candles on the sink and sit on the toilet (with the lid down) or on a chair. To replicate the watery environment of the tub, place a stone in the sink and open the faucet so you can hear it drip. Alternately, play a tape of nature sounds that includes the patter of rain. You can also perform the meditation when it is actually raining outside, so you can hear the drops falling on your roof.

Choose to take your bath at a time when your children, spouse, siblings, or mother-in-law aren't likely to disturb you. If necessary, unplug the phone. Reserve a half hour in the tub and fifteen minutes after bathing to complete the meditation.

Purchase two blue votive candles. If you can find sandalwood-scented votives, go for those first; in this meditation, the scent is more important than the candle color. Affix the candles in votive holders, light them, and place them on either side of the faucets on the tub ledge. If you're really enthusiastic about this meditation you can draw on a piece of cardboard the symbol of a crescent moon (the moon is related to the concept of water). Paint it silver, cut it out, and tape it to the wall at the end of the tub so you face it when you lie back.

Draw a warm bath (98 to 105 degrees), and add some of the

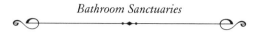

bath oil to the water. Position your bath pillow in the tub to support your neck and head. If you don't have a pillow, make one by folding a soft towel. Get into the tub, lie back, and luxuriate.

Let your gaze turn from time to time to the lighted candles. If any issue that's currently bothering you comes to mind, mentally "grab" and "thrust" it deep into the water. Sometimes an idea of how to solve your problem will occur while you're watching the candles. In this case, "capture" the possible solution in your mind's eye and "stick" it onto the candle. Go on to your next thought and repeat the process.

Eventually no more thoughts will occur to you. This means your mind and body have profoundly relaxed. This thoughtless, stress-free state is what you're aiming to achieve. You can't force relaxation. It just happens. If you don't feel totally at ease after thirty minutes, don't fret! Trust that the essences in the bath water are working subtle changes on your body, your chakras, which in Kundalini yoga are the spiritual nerve centers that align with the central nervous system, and on your aura, which is the psychic energy field or invisible emanation that is alleged to surround people, plants, animals, and inanimate objects.

When the time is up, step out of the tub. Before leaving, pull the plug on the water. As you dry off, visualize your troubles flowing down the drain with the bath water. Carefully carry the lighted votives to your room and place them on your bedroom altar.

Write in a notebook the possible solutions to your problems that occurred to you in the bath. If you've forgotten some of the ideas already, for inspiration look at the candles where you "stuck" your solutions. Don't be distressed if you still don't remember. The answers may appear in a dream or in another bath.

Occasionally refer back to your bath solutions notebook. You'll be amazed at how, over time, you've managed to come up with the right ways to solve your problems. Thank whatever higher power you believe in for the insights, and extinguish the candle flames with a snuffer. Aren't you happy you made time to take a bath?

I hope you're relaxed, rested, and ready, because in the next chapter we're going to get moving again, cleaning, organizing, and creating a sanctuary in your kitchen.

Chapter 6

The Sacred Kitchen

Kitchens are more than convenient places to quickly prepare and eat meals. In feng shui, the Chinese art of living well by creating balance in your environment, the kitchen represents the heart of the household, the center of its vital force. In days gone by, kitchens were centers of domestic activity. The entire family gathered around the hearth to enjoy a meal, hash over the day's events, and spin yarns late into the night. Often the kitchen was the warmest room in the house because of the constantly burning hearth fire. Therefore, it doubled as a nursery, a schoolroom, and even a bedroom at times.

The homemaker has always held undisputed reign over the kitchen precinct, and I'm no exception to that rule. My husband doesn't even know where the pots are kept! All sorts of superstitions have evolved around the cook and the kitchen.

Here's a variation on the adage, "Too many cooks spoil the broth," taken from my own experience.

When I was living in Scotland, I stayed in the home of a widower. One night, I prepared dinner for him and several guests. This tradition-bound gentleman wouldn't allow anyone to be in the kitchen with me while I was cooking. He told me that when he was a child, his mother had laid down this rule. Continual comings and goings in the kitchen disturbed her concentration and might cause her to spoil an entire meal—something unthinkable for the penny-wise Scots. To me, this attitude showed ultimate respect for a person's private space.

In my own home, I'd say "fat chance" to the opportunity of ever getting enough peace and quiet to prepare a meal without interference. Everything, including the proverbial kitchen sink, ends up parked in this room, from snow skis and Halloween costumes to power drills and kitty litter. The refrigerator, to put it kindly, stores many fond memories of past meals, some of those meals from the very distant past. The front of this "anthropological artifact" is plastered with reminder notes, children's artwork, restaurant coupons, and postcards from friends who've traveled to exotic places. Nevertheless, my kitchen is a warm, lively room that is often filled with friends and loved ones engaged in lively discussions. After the house quiets down at night, I often sit at the kitchen table in blissful solitude, sipping a cup of chamomile

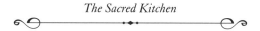

tea, and contemplate the day's events and even maybe the meaning of life.

LEARNING FROM
THAI DINING TRADITIONS

If your kitchen is as much the center of family activity as mine is, you still can make it a warm and friendly place that will appeal to everyone. The people of Thailand have a few tips to offer when it comes to creating comfortable dining spaces. They seek harmony and pleasure in everything they do, and they especially value hospitality. For example, when you visit Thailand, people constantly ask you if you're feeling well, by which they mean, "Are you happy?" To the Thais, a measure of happiness is to never go hungry, and this is why many of their important customs revolve around food and eating.

Thais don't have scheduled mealtimes. Instead, they eat little meals throughout the day and evening, so the dining area sees a lot of action. In spite of the fact that most of their dining rooms are open at the sides to let the refreshing breezes pass through, elaborate room arrangements, table decorations, and food presentation give the area a cozy feel.

Food is served on a long, teakwood table that stands only about a foot off the ground. Meals require hours of preparation, partly because of the care taken to make fancy presentations.

Dishes are arranged on very small plates, often made of china in celadon green. The delicate color resonates harmoniously with nature, which is important to Thais. Eating implements are made from bronze and are artfully tucked into folded napkins. Vases overflowing with flowers, like lotus and orchids, add a delicate wash of color to the setting. For a dinner party, the family may hire musicians, who sit in the background, playing wooden xylophones and flutes, and sing. Because the room is open-air, and because Buddhist temples abound everywhere, people also dine to the background sounds of chanting monks. Even when the sounds are of traffic in the streets, Thais don't mind because they consider street noise part of the natural rhythm of life. The Thai dining room, indeed, marks an intimate sacred space that all can share.

Obviously most people in our hectic, contemporary Western societies aren't going to take the time to make the complex meal preparations that the Thais do. However, in order to help create a harmonious place where your family can share some sacred space, perhaps you can take some hints from the Thais. Your dining area in the kitchen probably isn't open-air, but on a hot evening, you can make your kitchen mobile and serve dinner on the patio, balcony, or even in the backyard, just to make a fun change for everybody. After all, even though the kitchen is your dining Central Station, it doesn't have to be that way every day. A teakwood table in the kitchen may not fit your budget or decorating plan, and most Westerners find folding their legs under these kinds of tables uncomfortable anyway. But you can modify the idea, perhaps, by purchasing a long, solid oak table with wide, comfortable matching armchairs. This will encourage family members to relax, and perhaps dally over their meals to discuss the day's events, or talk about what's on their minds. When I was living in Britain, I noticed that many families, whether they lived in a country manor house or in a small city apartment, strived to have a big, solid table in the kitchen specifically for family gatherings.

As I mentioned, the Thais make elaborate food presentations and table decorations and put together small meals. You may not have time for intricate preparations, but even a small frozen dinner served on pretty china makes a more appealing meal. If the vegetables are artfully arranged on a pretty plate instead of on a microwavable plastic plate, little Janie just might eat them.

As to decorations, even plastic knives, forks, and spoons can be appealing when skillfully tucked into a napkin folded into the shape of a swan or a pocket, and this arrangement only takes a few minutes to create. A bouquet picked from the garden or a vase of dried flowers can also improve the dining environment. And don't forget fragrance: A glass bowl full of water and floating vanilla or cinnamon-scented candles is alleged to create a harmonious ambiance conducive to happy social interaction.

As to music, while the Thais listen to the bells and chanting from the monasteries, you could play a favorite family CD or turn the radio to a "mostly music" station. Avoid talk programs and television, or your family will tend to listen or watch rather than communicate with each other. So you see, you can take the Thai model and adapt it to your individual needs, budget, and time constraints.

TRANSFORMING YOUR KITCHEN

Transform your kitchen into a sacred space in progress. I say "in progress" because it probably goes through various incarnations from clean, tidy, and reverent to cluttered, messy, and just plain dirty. When you feel the need to "reclaim the sacred," here's what to do.

Your first step is—you guessed it—to tidy up really well. Always sweep the floor with a broom because in many cultures, brooms stand for spiritual cleansing. Next, wash the floor with vinegar and water. Besides being an effective cleaner, vinegar is supposed to purify spiritually. In the Voodun religion, the power of vinegar to physically clean an environment is assumed by analogy to also give it the power to purify spiritually. Thus, temple floors are washed with vinegar and water to chase away evil spirits and impure thoughts. If you are feeling especially enthusiastic, sprinkle a mixture of salt and water on the floor, cabinets, stove, sink, table, and chairs to further cleanse the space.

Weather permitting, open the window and a door, and if possible, freshen things up with flowers from the garden. Hang herbs to dry in the high space over the sink. Burn a stick of "culinary" incense like cinnamon, vanilla, orange blossom, or clove, and light scented candles. When you want to add a special touch, place an open bowl of fragrant potpourri on the counter. Try a trick a real estate friend once told me about. She said that when your house is on the market, you should throw a few fresh orange, lemon, or tangerine peels into the disposal and grind them up. It will give the kitchen a sweet, citrus scent that eliminates cooking odors and lends a cozy feel to the kitchen.

Refrigerator Art

A perfect way to personalize your kitchen, and create an activity for the entire family, is to use the outside of your refrigerator. I've already mentioned what my refrigerator door looks like, but you may object to such a topsy-turvy, unorganized approach. Some kitchen decorator consultants advocate keeping the outside of your refrigerator free from clutter so that, symbolically, you are encouraged to maintain a clutter-free kitchen as well. Others recommend that you simply attach one item to the refrigerator door—such as a picture of a goal you wish to achieve, or a beautiful landscape, so you can focus on the picture every time you open the fridge door. After all, with the exception of your main entrance, this door is probably the most used in your house. If you like to meditate in your kitchen, this is an especially useful idea.

Others like to personalize their refrigerators to such an extent that an entire category of "Refrigerator Art" has emerged over the last few years. Kids' Refrigerator Art competitions, whether drawn on paper and attached to the refrigerator, or painted on the appliance, are becoming popular. Connoisseurs of adult Refrigerator Art have paid up to $5,000 for prime examples. In San Diego, the Institute for Arts Education even conducts classes on Refrigerator Art for children to foster their creativity. Personalizing your refrigerator with artwork may be a fun project for your entire family to engage in to create a meaningful, communal sacred space.

KITCHEN SUPERSTITIONS

All sorts of superstitions in cultures worldwide have evolved around cooks and their kitchens. The Hindus treat their kitchen as the most hygienic area of the house because to do otherwise might incur the wrath of their gods. They even remove their shoes before entering the sacred precinct of the kitchen. Before dining, they sprinkle water around the room in remembrance of their ancestors.

If you want to perform a variation on this tradition, try dipping a clean dishtowel in rosewater, orange water, or any other pleasantly scented water. Then wave the towel around the room to distribute the droplets. You'll "sanctify" your kitchen and make it smell good in the bargain.

Another kitchen custom hails from the Candomblé religion practiced in Brazil. In this tradition, the cook is not allowed to prepare a meal within twenty-four hours of having sexual relations or when she is menstruating, as these activities are considered unclean. She also must remember to stir the pot clockwise, never counterclockwise, in order to bring the meal in balance with the rhythms of nature. This action is meant specifically to mimic the direction in which the sun is perceived to be passing through the heavens.

The cook also sings sacred songs while preparing the meal in order to obtain the gods' blessings. When the meal is prepared, the cook retreats from the room, never turning her back on the food, to show her respect for it. While I don't advocate that you prepare your meals in this way, I do think that if you whistle a merry tune while you work, or play the radio or a CD, your culinary tasks will probably pass more swiftly and happily.

If your kitchen is as disorganized as mine, there is an old English tradition you can follow to assure that activity in your kitchen hums like a well-oiled machine. Take a white saucer and place a piece of bread on it. Pour honey over the bread and soak it in milk, then place the plate on the stove. This is an offering to the "Hob," a kind of house fairy. Although this might sound like something you would never try, you might think again if you are preparing a Thanksgiving dinner for twenty people and want everything to work seamlessly.

So many superstitions have evolved around food it would take an entire book to list them all. That so many exist attests to the importance in our lives of food and the place where it is prepared. For example, to drop a knife spells bad luck, but if you drop a spoon and it lands upside down, it means a surprise is about to happen. Stirring the pot clockwise brings good fortune, but if you stir counterclockwise, you're in for a bad time. Spilled milk, especially on the threshold, is alleged to attract fairies, and you should never throw away a piece of bread unless you want your luck to go into the trash with it.

There are even so-called lucky foods associated with each month of the year. They include black-eyed peas in January, noodles in February, edible seeds in March, eggs in April, yogurt in May, cake in June, watermelon in July, corn in August, oysters in September, pumpkin pie in October, turkey in November, and fruit in December. Probably many of these lucky food superstitions developed because of seasonal availability of certain foods or their associations with different holidays.

USING THE KITCHEN AS A SACRED SPACE

Now that that I've inspired you to scrub your kitchen until it beams like a sunny summer morning, here's a suggestion on how to use it as a sacred space. As you've probably guessed, I'm a big fan of meditation. I find that even fifteen minutes of meditation a day clears my mind, helps me solve problems, opens my inner life to creativity and spirituality, and—according to my husband, anyway—immensely improves my humor! Here's an idea for a meditation you can perform in your kitchen during those quiet times.

Apple Juice Meditation

You'll need two blue tapers and candleholders, a stick of cinnamon incense and an incense burner, matches, and a clear glass filled with apple juice. For once, I recommend you don't use organic juice, because it can look muddy in the glass. For this meditation, you want clear liquid. Apples were sacred to the Druids, those ancient Celts who believed this fruit imparted great knowledge and wisdom.

Place the glass of juice in front of you on the kitchen table with the candles on either side of it. Put the incense burner in a convenient spot, where you don't have to breathe in the smoke directly. Light the tapers and the incense.

Take a comfortable seat in an upright chair in front of the glass, and fix your gaze on the cup. Immerse your thoughts in the amber liquid. Imagine that the wetness and freshness of the juice is covering you like the water from a pristine sea. Don't drink the juice yet, but mentally taste its sweetness.

Visualize yourself diving deep into the liquid, swimming like a fish along the ocean floor. As you glide effortlessly through this fathomless, silent sea, take a look at the marine life that has materialized around you—starfish on the bottom of the ocean bed, colorful seaweed and fish swimming soundlessly through the depths.

Eventually you arrive at a subterranean castle fashioned from barnacles, shells, and bits of ship rope. A lovely mermaid with flowing, blond hair and deep blue eyes appears in the doorway and beckons to you. Swim to her, and ask her to guide you on the path to inner knowledge. Listen to her message.

After a few minutes' communion with the mermaid, thank her for her wise counsel. Then turn and glide out of the sea castle and back home. Slowly float to the surface of the water, as if emerging from a deep pool. Presto! You're back in your kitchen once more. Drink the apple juice from the cup to refresh yourself. Write any messages you received in your journal.

Journaling in
Your Kitchen Haven

Journaling is an activity I find particularly fulfilling. It nourishes my mind and my spirit. Maybe that's why I like to do it in the kitchen, usually late at night when the rest of the household has gone to bed. There's something about the ticking clock, humming dishwasher, clean, damp dishes drying on the rack, and the smells of coffee or tea brewing (and maybe that piece of leftover pie on the table!) that excites me to write.

Many people, including me, have a hard time sometimes deciding what to write about, or keeping up with their journals, or even working up the enthusiasm to start writing. For those of you who are going through a rough patch of "journaler's block," I've concocted a few recipes. The ingredients are alleged to exert a positive influence on a person's thought patterns. If we truly are what we eat, maybe these potions will help you out, no matter where you decide to do your journaling. At the very least, you'll have whipped yourself up a tasty treat.

POTIONS FOR BODY AND SOUL

In this section, you will find a set of recipes for liquid refreshments designed to enhance creativity and inspiration for journaling, intuition, and concentration for meditation, and to help give you feelings of fulfillment, well-being, and tranquility so you can relax and feel perfectly at ease in your sacred space. Included are recipes for a juice, a soup, a shake, and a sauce.

JOURNAL JUICE
Mix together the following ingredients and drink for inspiration:

½ cup pomegranate juice (pomegranates are associated with
fertility of body and mind as well as the concept of
renewal)
¼ cup tangerine juice (tangerines symbolize zest for life and
inspiration)
¼ cup pineapple juice (pineapples stand for perfection)
½ teaspoon lemon balm (lemon balm aids self-expression
through writing)

MELLOW MUSHROOM SOUP
*Mushrooms can also help nudge you over the journal entry hump
because they are alleged to promote communicative abilities. The
following is one of my favorites, but if you have a special mush-
room soup recipe of your own, feel free to use it.*

1 pound fresh mushrooms, sliced
2 teaspoons lemon juice (lemons are alleged to refresh and
stimulate the mind)
1 cup water
4 tablespoons butter
1 teaspoon salt

½ teaspoon ground black pepper

2 tablespoons dry sherry (sherry can make you loquacious)

1 chicken bouillon cube

2 tablespoons flour

2 cups milk

2 carrots, thinly sliced (carrots are believed to bring good luck)

2 leeks, chopped (leeks are thought to help you keep a clear head)

1 tablespoon fresh dill, chopped (dill strengthens resolve, perhaps to help you stick to keeping a journal)

1. In a saucepan, melt 2 tablespoons of the butter over medium heat. Add the mushrooms, lemon juice, water, and bouillon cube, and cook until mushrooms are just tender. Set aside in a bowl.

2. Melt the rest of the butter in a pot. Add the leeks and carrots; sauté for 5 minutes. Stir in the flour until blended. Then stir in the milk, mushrooms, and sherry. Add salt and pepper to taste.

3. Reheat and serve. Garnish with fresh dill, if desired.

Shake Up Creativity

This formula is designed to enhance your intuition and creativity, both of which help you resonate with your inner being—and shake you up!

½ pint coconut ice cream (coconut is alleged to confer
strength and enhance creativity)
1 cup (8 ounces) canned, crushed pineapple (perfection)
¾ cup light cream
3 ounces frozen tangerine juice (half of a 6-ounce can—save
the rest to make juice to add a little gusto to your life—
tangerines stand for inspiration and zest)
1 small banana (bananas lend energy to your creative
endeavors)
½ cup ice cubes
¼ cup shredded coconut

1. Blend all the ingredients in a blender until smooth.
2. If you wish, garnish with toasted, shredded coconut and a
fresh rose (the rose is included for harmony and balance).

SAGE CHOCOLATE SAUCE

Can anything so sinfully delicious as chocolate help you obtain wisdom? Of course it can! The Maya Indians considered chocolate a food of the gods. They believed that eating it facilitated meditation and brought a person closer to the All-One. Who am I to disagree with ancient Mayan wisdom? Here's an ice cream topping recipe. Pour it on apple or almond ice cream, as both these botanicals are also thought to confer wisdom. If you eat vanilla ice cream, the vanilla will help you gain peace of mind; if you pour the sauce over cinnamon ice cream, you may improve your memory.

¾ cup whipping cream
½ cup butter
¼ cup sugar
6 ounces unsweetened chocolate, chopped into pieces
2 tablespoons water (if you prefer an alcoholic potion,
    substitute 2 tablespoons crème de cacao)

1. Heat the cream with the butter and sugar in the top of a double boiler. Stir until smooth.
2. Beat in the chocolate until melted.
3. Add the water a little at a time, and blend until smooth. Pour over the ice cream and serve.

Regretfully, we must leave this scene of high indulgence in wisdom and move on to other indoor sacred spaces. So why don't you pick up that bowl of ice cream and follow along?

Chapter 7

Other Indoor Sanctuaries

So far, we've taken a look at some of the more typical places where people locate their sacred spaces. Now we'll consider some other spaces within the home. If your house is short on space, or if it's not convenient to locate your sanctuary in your bedroom, bathroom, or kitchen, you might consider other areas of your home. Rooms like your home office or even your living room can easily be converted into a haven. These days, the trend has been to take more work home and even to establish one's business at home. While family members and friends may feel free to roam around most of the rest of the house, most people understand that the home office is a sacrosanct precinct to its occupant. So without hurting anybody's feelings, you can easily convert this area into a sanctuary where you will not be disturbed. Because everybody's work is different, you will naturally want to personalize your office in a way that accommodates the kind of work you do there.

HOME OFFICES

Here's what two people did to personalize a home office. As you read their stories, you will notice that some of the things they have done are very similar while others are very different. Their choices reflect their unique personalities, attitudes, and needs in their sacred spaces. Perhaps you can resonate with some of their ideas and incorporate them into your own home office.

Gregory's Den

A friend of mine chose to make a home office his sacred space. Gregory is a professor of Spanish at a local university. His home office has become more than a place to do work; it is an expression of his passionate intellectual interests and his travels. Although he probably wouldn't use this word to describe it, Gregory has turned the rough wood mantle over the stone fireplace in his office into a kind of altar that reflects his interest in Latin American and Southwestern culture as well as his travels abroad.

On Gregory's mantle is an authentic ancient Peruvian earthenware *moche* pot and two Chinese teapots colored in earthy, pale orange shades. An elegant reproduction statue of the Aztec rain god rubs shoulders with a Southwestern kachina doll. Two African candles and holders flank the ends of the mantle. Their intricate patterns—rendered in yellow, turquoise, red, green, and blue—lend a flash of color to the collection. Above the mantle, an eighteenth-century French costume-ball mask of a ram, worked in rich, brownish-red leather, stares boldly from the wall across the room to the door at anyone who dares cross the threshold. All these objects are either gifts or legacies. Whenever his gaze lights on his mantle, Gregory feels surrounded by the love of his friends and companions.

As much as he loves contemplating his mementos, Gregory has devised a way to create a purposeful, physical separation from them. His desk faces the wall opposite the mantle and window, and the relaxation area of the office is in front of the fireplace. This division makes his home office conducive to productivity as well as relaxation.

Gregory's home office faces southwest and commands a picture-perfect view of the front range of the Colorado Rockies, lending the room a den-like feel. He has taken advantage of the fireplace and the picture window to create a break area. There, he's grouped an overstuffed suede chair and matching brown sofa, a butcher-block table, and a large, red-and-black, Southwestern Indian rug. On a winter's day, he often relaxes on the couch and listens to his favorite Spanish flamenco music or Italian opera. Sometimes he catches forty winks there, too.

When he tires of looking at the mountains, he turns his eye to the Shaker bench in front of the window, on top of which he's set up a table fountain with pebbles and living bamboo. Two bonsai grace the sides of the fountain, and on the end of the bench, a cheery, orange amaryllis—a gift from his daughter—smiles at the sun. When it's time to go back to work, Gregory turns his back on the beauty so he doesn't get distracted.

Gregory's sacred space also reflects his other passion—books. In fact, two walls of his study are lined from floor to ceiling with books. Gregory explains, "When I'm surrounded by my books, I feel comforted. There's also something about the sight and smell of my books that excites my imagination and encourages me in my work. I never feel my office is my own space until my books are ensconced in it."

Rather than letting this room evolve, Gregory established the den all at once because he needed to have his office functional right away. His advice to anyone contemplating setting up a similar sanctuary is to make lots of room for books. He informs me that he finds it convenient to have everything in one place because he is constantly consulting his books. If he had to hunt all over the house, he'd waste too much time.

Vicki's Eyrie

Vicki is a middle-school teacher turned crime-fiction writer. She chose an enclosed sun porch for her office because she claims

she's a solar powered kind of gal who needs a lot of light to stimulate her creativity. The sun porch provides plenty of sunshine
and fresh air, and the eighty-foot blue spruce outside the bank of
windows serves as a natural focal point for the room. The quality
of the light is also important to Vicky, so she painted the walls a
creamy yellow shade and sanded down the hardwood floors.
She's acquired an old, flat, yellow pine desk without drawers that
suits her just fine because the color matches the rest of the room.

Vicki believes that two ingredients essential for a home
office, besides light, include having something alive and
vibrant in the room and using a bit of humor. She loves the
feeling that the spruce tree outside the window gives her of
being inside and outside at the same time. With the squirrels
clambering up and down the trunk and the flocks of chattering
birds that make their homes in the branches, she sometimes
fantasizes that she's living in an aviary. The sounds and sights
of nature stimulate her imagination and revitalize her so she
can produce her best work. She decorated the inside of the
room with plants, just as many of the other people interviewed
for this book have done, to bring even more life into the room.

A writer's lair can sometimes be a seriously dreary place,
in spite of a person's best efforts to decorate it in light colors
and use a lot of light. To add an infusion of humor, Vicki has
pinned a picture of ducklings lined up behind their mother on
her office bulletin board and written under it "Time to go for a
waddle" to remind her to exercise.

Rita's Yoga Room

Perhaps your job doesn't require a home office, but you may enjoy other interests and want to pursue them in your sanctuary. My friend Rita is a museum curator, yoga enthusiast, and rock collector. She's in the process of converting the front room of her home into a place where she can practice yoga, meditate, display some of the items she's collected from her career in the museum field, and work at her current job.

Rita claims that she can't do yoga just anywhere. She needs a place to retreat from the stresses that build up in her daily life. She also feels that a yoga room needs certain trappings, like pillows, splashes of color, plants, light, scents, music, and a meditation area. Since her space is limited, she has chosen to make her home office a combination workplace and yoga room.

Because yoga is an Asian practice, Rita's plan is to include representations of the five Chinese elements. She has plants and figurines, as well as the desk where she works, to stand for the element wood, and she has gemstones to symbolize earth. For water, she has set a female Shiva in water. She also intends to have a brass cauldron, which she will fill with fresh spring water every day for inspiration for her job. The fire element is represented by the fireplace in the room and the candle that she keeps burning in the center of a quartz crystal ring. Wind, or air, comes from an incense brazier, and she may hang a wind chime later. She thinks symbols of the elements will help balance her chakras, that is to say, the energy centers in her body, and help

her work more efficiently. She still does not know what she will choose to represent the Chinese element metal, but she is certain something appropriate will find its way to her. Unlike Gregory, she considers her yoga room and office a work in progress.

She says that eventually she will hang her masks from Malaysia, Bali, and the Philippines on one of the walls. Right now, she has put up a Haitian Voodoo Baron Samedi flag. This flag is made from red and black sequins that shimmer in the sunshine. In her opinion, the colors speak to the essence of her being.

When I asked if she minded that her sacred space is the first room a person sees on entering the home, she replied, "Not at all. The room feels welcoming and all-embracing and I want visitors to feel welcome. If people feel welcome, the conversations that take place in the room will be stimulating and enjoyable, and further energize the room."

Rita's comment suggests an idea put forth in Chapter 1, that boundaries are important not only for what they exclude, but also for what they include. The point at which the boundaries meet, whether it be in a kitchen or a yoga room, can produce new ways of looking at the world that can energize spaces.

A LIVING ROOM SHELF SANCTUARY

Now that I've run through the "usual suspects" for home sanctuaries, I'm going to surprise you with a location you may not have thought of—your living room. Even though the living room is often the most communal room in the house, that doesn't have to stop you from carving out a sacred space in this public location. A quick and space-efficient option is to establish an altar on a living room shelf. According to interior decorators, built-in living room shelves are becoming a hot request for custom-built houses, and homeowners who are looking for more storage space and getting weary of staring at white walls.

One way to turn a living room shelf into a personal space is to use it to reflect your philosophy of life or ethnic background. That's what a Russian woman I know did. In her country of origin, the color red holds a great deal of significance. In fact, the words "red" and "beautiful" are one and the same. So, Red Square and the Red Army actually mean "Beautiful Square" and "Beautiful Army."

To celebrate her cultural heritage, Tanya has collected Russian crafts colored predominantly in red. She's arranged an attractive display of the pottery, dolls, painted spoons, and embroidered cloths on her living room shelf. Her goal has been to find something in every known shade of red—with astounding results. Anyone who enters her living room is immediately taken by the elaborate tableau, and this usually leads to a discussion of Russian traditions.

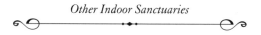

THRESHOLD CUSTOMS FROM AROUND THE WORLD

With the world's burgeoning population and the way most societies are increasingly oriented toward city life, the need to establish a boundary between the privacy of the home and the outside world is felt even more acutely. This is so even for nonEnglish-speaking cultures, where communal living and dwelling in close proximity is habitual.

Houses are creeping closer together in new American suburban developments, and within city centers it's the rare household that doesn't share at least one wall. Pedestrians and vehicles overflow in the streets, and it seem that prying eyes are everywhere. No wonder so many homes crouch behind enormous garages, six-foot fences, and landscaping constructed from large bushes, evergreens, and thorny plants.

Despite these efforts, our interior home space is rarely free from intrusions. Telemarketers, television ads, advertising that comes in over the fax line, and computer spam bombard us every minute of the day. People in other parts of the world have created unique ways to create a boundary between their homes and the outside world. Perhaps you can pick up some tips on how to strengthen the boundary of your own threshold.

Chinese Door Guardians

Chinese mythology is filled with spirit guides, including door guardians. Carved from red-colored peach wood, images and figures of these protective gods were hung on the front gate to drive away ghosts, wild beasts, and human intruders. In modern times, people have grown less concerned with ghosts, wild animals, and other terrifying aspects of the environment. They have turned their attention to improving quality of life.

The peach-wood door guardians have been transformed into red paper banners painted with symbols of protection. At the New Year's festival, Chinese householders may write wishes for good luck and prosperity on their door banners, often in the form of couplets. A colleague of mine from China informs me that as part of the legacy of the Mao era, banners are often strung over the doorways of restaurants as well as homes to express the owner's political sentiments or philosophy of life.

Crossing the Threshold

Another Chinese custom dictates that it is impolite for a visitor to tread on a host's threshold, as it is believed that such behavior shows disrespect for sacred space. This is reflective of an unspoken tradition I noticed when I lived in Britain. There, everyone puts a bristly doormat outside the front door, even if they live in apartments. As many people know, it rains a lot in England, and the mats are there for visitors and occupants to wipe their feet. But that isn't the most interesting part of this unspoken custom—it's the visitors' behavior. Whether it's raining or the sun has shone for a week, whether their shoes are dirty or just out of the shoebox, all visitors automatically pause at the threshold and vigorously wipe their shoes on the mat. Perhaps this represents an awareness, albeit unconscious, that the other person's home is a sacred space.

We have doormats in the United States as well, but ours come in a variety of designs and pictures, some with humorous sayings written on them. Like Chinese red banners, our doormats are probably more an expression of the home's occupants than a way to clean shoes. I've noticed that most visitors to my house actually step over the mat into the front hall. Or, if the weather is foul, they only wipe their shoes in a perfunctory manner. Nobody does as assiduous a job as the British. I can only conclude that "mat wiping" in Britain is a way to show respect for the host's inner sanctum.

First Footing in Scotland

The topic of feet on thresholds reminds me of a wonderful Scottish (and Irish) custom called "first footing." The first person over the threshold on New Year's Day is supposed to be a harbinger of the kind of luck the household will experience throughout the year. If the visitor has dark hair, the luck will be good. This superstition harkens back to the days of the Viking raids. The one person you didn't want to see at your door was a blond Norseman decked out in a helmet with upraised sword, hell-bent on pillage and destruction.

Nowadays at the New Year's celebration (called Hogmany), dark-haired men are much in demand. Soon after the stroke of midnight, the dark-haired first-footer appears at the door bearing a lump of coal for the hearth, sometimes a bagful of fragrant herbs, a pinch of salt, and always kisses for the occupants. As a token of gratitude, the householder invites him to join the festivities, which often consists of dancing Highland flings, eating holiday delicacies, and imbibing more than one wee dram of fine whiskey. Eventually, the first-footer is sent on his way, often with a gift bottle of malt, to arrive at the next house, and so on, until dawn breaks. As to the superstition about the luck the first footer brings, I think that he's the lucky one in this scenario with all the gifts and attention he receives.

Carrying the Bride

Probably the British threshold custom that's "carried the most weight" with cultures worldwide is the tradition where the groom carries the bride over the threshold. Nobody knows its exact origin. Some say that in the old days, the young maiden, reluctant to lose her virginity, had to be carried, lest she run away. Somehow I doubt this theory! Others postulate that the groom carries to bride either to keep her safe from mean-spirited elves that hide under everybody's threshold, or to prevent her from stumbling on the threshold and bringing bad luck to the marriage.

Who knows if any of these superstitions is true? All I know is my husband carried me over our threshold, and I found the experience incredibly romantic. I consider thresholds to be boundaries that divide places I've been to and have yet to go as well as events that have happened and those yet to occur. Therefore, I feel that being carried over my first threshold sweetly and ceremonially marked my transition from single to married life.

PROTECTING YOUR THRESHOLD

If you want to do something physical to protect your threshold, here are some ideas collected from cultures worldwide. You can choose to work with any of these suggestions, depending on your inclinations. Even if you're not concerned with protecting your threshold, you'll enjoy reading what other people through the ages have done with their front doors.

Celtic Hole Stones

In ancient times, the Celts set great store by stones with holes in them. They named them luck stones (*an cloc cosanta*).

The stones ranged in size from as small as a necklace charm to megaliths. The large boulders are usually found near the thresholds of stone circles. It is thought that their purpose was to protect, heal, and enhance personal psychic powers; seal marriages, by having the couple pass through the hole in the stone; and help ease the journey of those who had passed on into the afterlife by passing the corpse through the stone. The smaller stones were either worn as necklaces or buried beneath the threshold.

Protective Objects to Bury

Over time, many botanicals and objects have been ascribed protective powers in the folklore of various cultures. If you ask me whether any of these measures work, I must be honest and reply that it largely depends on what you believe. If you're convinced that burying a bagful of sage and salt under your front porch will deflect negativity, it might just do that. If you're not a believer, the gesture probably won't work.

Other popular items to bury include two crossed needles or five new pennies, both of which are alleged to bring good luck. If you bury a bit of food under your front porch, it's said you'll never go hungry. If you try this last method, my advice is to bury the food deep enough that the raccoons won't get into it!

If you don't want to dig up around the doorstep, or if you live in an apartment, there are plenty of other things you can hang around the doorway to provide psychological protection.

Mezuzahs

In traditional Jewish homes, a case called a *mezuzah* is nailed to the doorpost. Inside the case, a tiny parchment scroll is handwritten in a special writing with a command from the biblical Book of Deuteronomy for the residents to keep God's word constantly in mind and heart. On the back of the scroll is written in Hebrew the first letter of one of the names of God. When a family moves into a new house, a short dedication ceremony is performed, which consists of reading a brief blessing and attaching the mezuzah to the right doorpost at an angle. (It's placed at an angle because evidently the rabbis couldn't agree on whether it should be affixed horizontally or vertically, so they compromised!) Every time the occupants pass through the door, they're supposed to touch the mezuzah and kiss their fingers to express respect and love of God.

Witch Balls

Witch balls are silver glass balls, popular in England and New England, suspended by the door to trap evil spirits and keep away people who would do the occupant harm. Originally witch balls had nothing to do with witches. These balls first appeared in Bohemia during the seventeenth century. This region was famous for its glassblowers. Around Christmas, the blowers would gather for a bit of holiday cheer.

Between quaffing tankards of ale, they competed to see who could blow the largest glass bubble before it broke.

The wives gathered up the balls and swished a solution of silver nitrate around the inside of the ornaments to give them a silvery sheen. Then, they sold the balls at the local Christmas bazaars as threshold decorations. Eventually the balls were exported to England and America, where somehow, people got the notion that the orbs were meant to keep evil at bay. The English-speaking world probably associated the balls with the holly boughs that they hung over their doors for protection.

Today you can find some lovely examples in New England antique shops. Ironically, many shopkeepers are loath to part with them because they believe their good luck will walk out the door with the witch ball. If you do manage to separate a shop owner from a ball, it'll be well worth the price. Whether or not you believe in the ball's protective forces, it will make a charming addition to your door décor—much more lovely than an old iron horseshoe!

Native American Measures

If you're drawn to Native American traditions, try keeping a bowlful of colorful turquoise by the front door to ward off negativity. Other items various Native American cultures keep near the threshold include a pink conch shell, red coral, and eagle feathers. Zuni women have been known to preserve a husband's footprint and keep it by the front door for times when he is away hunting or on other trips. The superstition is that if the footprint is kept in this way, the husband will come to no harm and will not be tempted to be unfaithful. Peruvian Indians hang the last, dried stalk and ear of corn over the doorway to invite the protection of the Corn Goddess.

African-American "Flash-and-Light"

The African-American Voodun tradition is rich with protective symbols for house, garden, and car. One of the measures taken against unwelcome visitors of flesh or spirit is to place burned-out light bulbs in a basket on the front porch. The effect is similar to the Voodun theory that mirrors reflect negativity back to the person who approaches with evil thoughts in mind. In this case, the Voodun practitioner places light bulbs by the door to deflect the negativity. Burned-out bulbs are chosen because people outside the faith usually disregard these seemingly useless objects. Practitioners also believe that the bulbs will light up on a higher, spiritual plane of existence, discharging the negative vibrations there.

Protection Botanicals

Before the advent of modern medicine, people relied exclusively on botanicals to cure their ills. Because of this, legends have grown around the power of certain herbs to protect as well as cure. For example, legend has it that you can sprinkle mustard seed or cayenne pepper on the doorsill to guard your home. These two botanicals might have acquired this reputation because of their strong flavor. If you don't sprinkle them for psychological protection, I've heard that they keep ants from crossing the threshold "like a charm." For a prettier botanical solution, plant marigolds, juniper, lilies, bamboo, or ferns around the front of the house, or grow them in pots on the porch.

You can also fill a little sachet bag with any combination of the following protection herbs: rosemary, basil, bay, sage, dill, cinquefoil, lavender, mint, rue, frankincense, cinnamon, mountain ash berries, and angelica. Tie the opening shut with a saucy red satin ribbon (red is for protection), and suspend the bag over your doorway. At the very least, the light, herby fragrance will freshen the front portion of your house and create a pleasant environment. I draw the line at one botanical—garlic. The bulbs are too pungent to have hanging around the front door. You might scare away your friends along with your enemies!

Chapter 8

Enchanted Gardens

'm going to rustle you out of the house and into the sunshine and fresh air. Ready? Grab your windbreaker and your mud boots, and let's go! In this chapter you're going to learn how to make a sanctuary in your garden or on your patio or balcony. You'll also read about solutions other cultures have come up with to create a sacred space outdoors.

MY IDEAL RETREAT

I once tried my hand at an all-white garden, that is, a garden teeming with white blossoms. I planted it in a twelve-by-fifteen-foot space with a birdbath as the centerpiece. I surrounded the perimeter with boxwoods, made entrances at the south and north, and laid bricks in a circular pattern around the fountain. I planted white-flowering crocuses, tulips, sweet-smelling hyacinths, and daffodils, along with white astilbe, viburnum, miniature rose bushes, and fragrant nicotiana. I added a magnolia bush for more scent and a dogwood tree for height.

I loved that garden, but when I look back, it didn't have two features I'd add now—a waterfall and a meditation bench. My tastes have also changed, and a garden of all one color doesn't excite me the way it once did. That's fine by me—most personal sacred spaces are supposed to be works in progress that change as you do.

Today, my ideal garden would be more colorful. I'd plant bunches of annuals, like marigolds, zinnias, petunias, and dahlias, and some perennials like Indian paintbrush, echinacea, blue flax, and red and yellow yarrow.

I'd also pay attention to scent because fragrances soothe the body, mind, and spirit. I'd haul out my big, potted jasmine during the summer months and surround myself with other scented flowers. The miniature roses of the white garden, which rarely emitted even the lightest scent, would give way to old-fashioned, musk-scented tea roses. I'd plant a variety of herbs, too, like lavender for its relaxing, fresh perfume, and piquant bergamot (the same herb that scents Earl Grey tea). I'd include citrus-like lemon balm and sweet creeping thyme, and probably a potted, fresh-scented rosemary that I'd also need to bring in during the coldest part of the winter, at least in this climate.

I'd include plants for healing, too, like chamomile as a tranquilizer, motherwort to alleviate female problems, purple coneflower, also called echinacea, to cure colds, and fennel to aid digestion. Culinary herbs, like basil, chive, sage, dill, marjoram, and parsley would overtake a corner of the garden because nothing compares to the taste of fresh herbs in home-cooked food.

I'd complete my dream garden with a wind chime tinkling sweetly in the background, a butterfly house, a hummingbird feeder, a bird feeder, and a birdhouse. Nothing lulls body and soul like watching little critters cavort around the landscape. This is my dream garden. What's yours?

THAI SPIRIT HOUSES

No matter what kind of garden you devise, you can enhance it with a "spirit house." This charming tradition hails from Thailand, where it's common practice to erect one of these little houses at the front gate. The teak structure looks like an elaborate birdhouse and sits atop a five-foot pole. Its shape mimics traditional Thai houses: an A-frame with open sides and a slanting roof with the ends turned up. The spirit house might hold sweet-smelling incense. The homeowner might also sometimes make offerings of food or coins for prosperity. Thai people believe that since such items make humans happy, these types of offerings will also please friendly spirits and attract them to the dwelling.

KIDS NEED SACRED SPACE, TOO

My friend Sara and her husband own a teahouse. They also have three small children. Since Sara blends the teas in a converted garage in the backyard, she hit on the idea to design a special garden where the children could play and she could keep an eye on them. She wanted to create a space with enough excitement to hold the kids' interest so she wouldn't have to drive them somewhere else everyday for recreation. She also needed a quiet retreat outside the house where she or her husband could occasionally take a few minutes to relax in private.

Since the children were fascinated with fairy tales and myths, she researched fairy henges. These circular gardens, usually built in the wild, are alleged to attract fairies. The outdoor location makes the children think they are cavorting in the wild, but at the same time keeps them feeling perfectly safe. Beyond the grassy backyard at the back of their lot, Sara constructed a nine-foot-diameter stone patio and bounded it with a moss-covered wall, low enough for the children to use as a seat. She allowed for some crannies in the walls for the kids to hide their secret little treasures or make offerings to the fairies.

Fairy henges are supposed to include representations of the four elements of nature—Air, Fire, Water, and Earth—at each of the compass points. In the east, Sara hung a wind chime to represent Air, and in the south she built an outdoor stone fireplace for the element Fire. A birdbath in the west provided the element of water, while in the north, she placed a geode for Earth. She also erected a totem pole to represent her family history. As to greenery, she planted a big mugwort bush in the east to block part of the view to the back of the house and help the children imagine they're playing in the wild. She positioned trees at the other cardinal points—a fir in the south, an apple in the west, and a rowan in the north. Potted plants, herbs, and bulbs, planted haphazardly around the space, enhance the feeling of wilderness. The landscaping not only adds ambiance but also serves the purpose of adding privacy. The plants Sara chose include St. John's wort for healing, catnip to calm nervous tension (and to make the family cat happy), peppermint and angelica to add to teas, sage as a culinary spice, and California poppy for its drought tolerance and color. The children have had their say in what should go into the garden, too. For example, Sara helped them construct a "fairy house," a space very much in progress, filled with tiny "fairy" plants such as lily of the valley, chamomile, fairy bells, nasturtium, miniature thyme, and even a cherry tomato plant.

Sara explains that part of the reason she created the garden was for her kids to understand where their food comes from and so that they could have the pleasure of seeing it grow within the boundaries of their sacred space. She also uses this sacred space to teach the children about the medicinal properties of herbs. She's left an area on the north side of the garden as a place where the children can let their imaginations run wild and plant any sort of garden they fancy. They tend the garden, harvest the crop, and make it into food for the table. For example, the kids have made roasted, salted sunflower seeds, raspberry and blackberry jams, and applesauce. This season they are putting in a pickle garden. In this way, the sanctuary also becomes a place for learning, personal growth, and experimentation.

During the summer in the evenings, the whole family gathers around the circle to toast marshmallows. Sara lights the candles, sits in front of the totem pole, and tells fairy tales. This space fulfills many functions. It's an untamed but safe haven in an urban setting where the children can play. It's a horticultural classroom, and it's also a sanctuary where the family can bond and create memories.

IBERIAN PATIO GARDENS

When I first came to the University of Colorado, I was fascinated with the architecture. Most of the buildings are constructed from yellow sandstone, with many arched windows fronted by wrought-iron balconies and covered by red-tiled roofs. To me, the style looked like a combination of a South-western hacienda and a medieval European fortress.

What enchanted me most, however, was the central quad behind the student union, with its spectacular, multiheaded fountain. Sunken directly in the center of the square, and accessible by several geometrically patterned sets of steps, it's a splendid place for students to gather on Colorado's many hot, bright days to cool off, chat, or study. Some of my fondest college memories were formed in that quad.

Only later, as I began to travel widely through southern Europe and Latin America, did I realize the architectural debt the quad owed to Iberian garden design. Iberian gardens reflect the influences of two cultures, the Roman and the Moorish, which held sway over the Iberian Peninsula (modern-day Spain and Portugal) for several centuries.

The Romans, who were in control from approximately 205 B.C. to A.D. 500, built their houses in a square around a patio called an atrium. In the center of the atrium was a water source, such as a fountain or a well. This style provided a way to enjoy the outdoors in seclusion and safety.

The Moors, who governed from 711 to 1492, added features in an effort to turn the patio into an indoor–outdoor garden that they called "heaven on earth." These gardens became sacred spaces for contemplation, meditation, and relaxation. Arbors covered with flowering vines provided both brilliant color and shady protection from the sun's searing rays. The ever-changing patterns of dappled sunlight and shade made for serene contemplation in every season of the year.

The Romans covered their interior patios with materials like tiles, stones, and bricks, but the Moors arranged them in elegant geometrical patterns. This same geometrical theme extended to fountain decoration, which was often ornamented with tiles in brilliantly colored designs. All was not stone and tile in the Moorish garden; potted orange and lemon trees, jasmine, roses, and hanging planters filled with riots of flowers lent color and fragrance to the scene. Irrigation canals running between garden and the interior furnished a primitive but successful kind of air conditioning. In later centuries, the Spanish and Portuguese incorporated features like herb gardens, which they learned to plant from Medieval monks, and topiaries and statues, an inheritance from Italian Renaissance and Neoclassical times.

Today's Iberian patio garden is a feast for the senses as well as a sanctuary of bliss. It provides a place to find a protected, restful retreat from the world and, importantly, a place to feel at one with the beauties of nature—in short, the perfect sacred space. The Spanish garden is a quintessential example of an outdoor retreat that stimulates the five senses yet is also restful and bucolic, a protected outdoor sanctuary for the occupant. Let Spanish gardens inspire you to perhaps incorporate some of these same features, such as colorful tiles, fountains, statues, topiaries, canals, and fragrant flowers into your outdoor sanctuary design.

HOW DIFFERENT CULTURES COMMUNE WITH NATURE

All this talk about dream gardens and carefully constructed sacred spaces is well and good, but if you live in an apartment complex in the middle of a busy city, it's not likely that you'll have room for a meditation garden or a fairy henge. What to do? Take a hike! Go out into nature, even if it's to the park down the street. Even the biggest cities have dedicated open space to be used as a refuge from the noise, traffic, concrete, and congestion of city life. St. James's in London, the Botanical Gardens in Denver, or Chapultepec Park in Mexico City are just a few examples of great sacred spaces. If you quiet yourself and pay attention, you'll be surprised how, even with a bunch of people milling around, the grasses and flowers, bushes, and especially the trees will speak to you. If you calmly meander or sit quietly in this sacred space, you will start to resonate with it, attuning yourself to the rhythms of nature.

Most of us live in a world where electricity transforms night into day. We can, and sometimes must, work and play around the clock. When we do this consistently, we fall out of sync with the natural rhythm of the planet. Entering into a rapport with nature helps ease our lives back into the natural cycle of things. This type of harmonious balance is what people strive to achieve in their sacred spaces. Here are some unusual ways people from cultures around the world and over time have chosen to form a rapport with their natural environments.

Hawaiian Waterfall Offerings

A favorite way to honor nature is to construct a temporary altar, a "one-time" sacred space in the trees, woods, meadows, mountains, streams, or by the seashore. When I vacationed in Maui last summer, I took a walk in the forest by a majestic waterfall. Plummeting down from a high mountain into a lush, tropical rainforest, the water ended up flowing into a deep, indigo-colored pool. Delicate orchids clung shyly to the densely spaced trees that surrounded the space, while bolder ivy and other vines shinnied up the trunks to make a green canopy overhead.

Pausing by the pool to admire its beauty, I spied evidence of recent human activity. A small statue of a goddess stood in the shallows on a stone ledge—of what deity, I have no idea. Several orchid leis lovingly encircled the figurine, mimicking the rings of water that formed in the pool. Clay dishes filled with fruit—pineapples, melons, and some fruit I didn't recognize—nuts, grilled fish, and Maui onions were set in front of the deity, as though she were dining at an Olympian feast. Such a perfect offering in an exquisite setting!

Sand Altars in Rio de Janeiro

Another version of a one-time altar I've seen hails from Brazil, where people gather once a year on the beach to honor Iemanjá, a traditional sea goddess. Every year on December 31, the entire city of Rio migrates to the beach. Families and friends gather and carve holes in the sand, which they fill with lighted candles and flowers. Some sand altars may commemorate a relative or friend who has died at sea or abroad. Others honor the mother goddess of Brazilian folk religion.

People also construct miniature wooden boats and trim them with flowers, combs, soaps, mirrors, and tiny bottles filled with sweet perfume. At midnight, as fireworks explode from atop the high-rise hotels to ring in the New Year, the faithful who are holding vigil on the beach below murmur prayers and launch their candlelit crafts into the sea. They top off the evening's festivities with a "purification bath" in the foaming surf. In this way, Brazilians—whether they're followers of the folk religion or not—commemorate the feast day of Iemanjá, the lithe Lady of the Vibratory Force of the Sea.

Living Trees As Altars

Before the Civil War, slaves who wanted to practice the religion of their African roots were forced to worship in secret. Since they had no way to make an altar to their gods, they ventured out into the garden or down by the fields late at night and offered prayers to their deities at a designated tree. In this, they followed a custom of their ancestors, who proffered prayers to tropical trees, such as the fig. By way of adapting to their new environment, the slaves chose a beech tree, an oak, or perhaps even a silver fir as a focal point for spiritual activities. In this way, the plantation owner never learned that his slaves worshipped their African gods right under his nose.

The Oldest Standing Stones

By chance, on a coach tour through the Scottish Highlands, I happened on the most stirring outdoor sanctuary I've ever seen. There were very few people on this tour, and as a consequence, we finished visiting the obligatory sites for the day with plenty of time to spare. Our guide scratched his chin, contemplating how to amuse us for another hour. At last, he told us he knew of a field nearby, where we could visit the oldest preCeltic stone circle in all the British Isles.

We agreed and set off for the ruins in a spirit of adventure. We were not disappointed. The field was tucked away off the beaten track. Enormous, lichen-covered gray stone boulders rose out of the mist to confront us like prehistoric sea creatures in an ocean of green. There was more than one stone circle and an area that looked like it had been the foundation of an ancient temple. Several monoliths stood like sentries guarding the field, and many of these stones were carved with worn, indecipherable markings.

I identified a huge hole stone, like those described in Chapter 7, that might have marked the entrance to a temple. The impossibly green, misted grass; the rough stones tinted in shades of gray that varied from brownish to almost blue; the whistling wind; and the salty taste of the breeze blowing up from the not-too-distant sea all combined to make the site a feast for the senses. This was a place where the imagination could run wild. In my opinion, if you were looking for the quintessential haven in nature, this would be the best you could find.

I don't remember the name of the site, nor can I verify that those were indeed Britain's oldest standing stones, but it doesn't make a difference. It was the ancient feel of the place that mattered, and the sense of holiness that still permeated the stones in that sacred space.

BRING THE FOREST HOME TO YOU

You can bring a taste of the wild wood home to you even if you don't see yourself making the journey to Maui or Scotland any time soon. A friend of mine lives in a condo with a west-facing balcony. In the summer, she puts out so many houseplants that the balcony looks like a verdant jungle. She hangs a sculpted sun on one wall and wooden flying geese on the other. On an end table, she sets up a tabletop fountain, and she strings her hammock nearby. The plants shelter the balcony from Colorado's searing summer sun, not to mention prying eyes of fellow condo dwellers, and they provide a perfect place for her to meditate, snooze, or read.

A Soul Tree to Guide You

You don't have to wait for spring to arrive to bring the outdoors inside. You can buy an indoor tree and make it into a personal "soul tree." This is also a fun activity for children, and caring for a living thing teaches them responsibility. Having a tree inside your home also imbues your inner sanctum with life.

A soul tree is a tree that grows with you as you mature in body, mind, and spirit. It is a being with which you can share your most intimate thoughts in a symbolic way. In this sense, the tree comprises a mini sacred space.

Choose a tree that fits your purpose. The following are particularly good choices: hazel for healing and wisdom, ash for prosperity and family unity, rowan for protection and inspiration, fir for strength, rosemary for remembrance, oak for beginnings, and apple for love and creativity.

You can pot a seedling or buy a small, prepotted tree available from most nurseries and gardening centers during the spring and fall. If you don't want to plant the tree outside because you think you may move, or if you don't have a garden or access to the countryside, select a Norfolk pine or a palm tree. They do well indoors and can travel with you.

Water and care for the tree in the usual fashion until the time comes to perform the blessing and dedication ceremony. If you've chosen an indoor tree, a good time to do this little ritual is around Christmas, Hanukkah, or the winter solstice, which is when the days begin to grow longer in the northern hemisphere. If this timing doesn't suit, perform the ceremony any time that accommodates the practices of your faith. If you're dedicating an outdoor tree, plant it around Arbor Day in northern climes. Before then, the ground is too frozen—the tree could die if planted in inclement weather. Believe me, there's nothing more depressing than to watch your soul tree go belly-up on you.

Plant the tree outside, or, if it's an indoor tree, put it in its permanent location. Decide in advance on a name for the tree. You can call it anything you want, but I recommend choosing something that indicates a quality you would like to cultivate in yourself. In my case, I've named more than one soul tree "Patience."

On a piece of parchment paper, write the tree's name in red ink and attach it with red thread to a branch. Declare aloud that by naming the tree, you have chosen it as your soul tree. Promise to care for it always, and ask that the blessings of the All-One be conferred upon it. Water the plant well.

If you prefer an already established tree, go to a large tree in your yard, a park, or the forest of any kind that I've mentioned, and greet it. Tell the tree your name, and ask if it will consent to be your tree friend. Then communicate the name you've selected for it. Take one of its fruits (nut, cone, or berry) and place it in a crevice or where two branches meet as a symbol of the bond between you. Take another fruit from the tree and bring it back home with you as a further symbol of the bond you have established. Go to this tree whenever you wish to be revitalized, to meditate, or just to talk. Always bring a water libation. Keep your tree trimmed of dead leaves and branches, and clean up the ground around it. At holidays like Christmas or Arbor Day, decorate your personal tree with strips of colorful cloth.

Chapter 9

A Home Away from Home

his chapter describes how to carve out a sacred space in an unfamiliar setting. In this particular section, we'll start by calling to mind how it feels when you've been traveling in another city, maybe even another country. You've spent all day at a conference, hitting up customers, or making a presentation. All you want is to go home and tumble into your warm, cozy bed.

Instead, you return to your "Chez Bland" hotel room, with a bed with a lumpy mattress, a room thermostat set to forty degrees in January, and hermetically sealed windows. The sterile bathroom overwhelms you with its antiseptic odor and fluorescent lighting, and you can't even manage to wrestle your clothes onto the theft-proof hangers.

DEBUG YOUR HOTEL ROOM

Even the smallest personal touches can make a hotel room feel like home. Rather than just bringing the barebones essentials of shampoo and makeup remover, pack one or two indulgent items, such as a packet of bubble bath or a miniature bottle of perfume. Set these out on the bathroom vanity to personalize your space.

Pack your "spiritual assistance essentials" in your traveling altar. Options for this can include a very small incense burner (I've seen some as little as two inches in diameter), a couple of sticks of incense for each day you'll be away, or scented candles to banish stale hotel smells. Try scents known to calm the nerves, such as lavender, or try a scent that reminds you of home. Do you live near the water? Then a fragrance that reminds you of the ocean would be appropriate. You can also bring a tiny totem, statue, or any other personal symbol that is comforting to you. Round out your traveling kit with a small book of devotional readings or meditations, a portable CD player, and a recording of nature sounds.

Bring something that reminds you of home—a rock from the garden, a shell from the ocean near your house, or a framed photograph of a loved one. Once when I was leaving home to spend a year in Britain, I plucked four ripe apples from the tree in my garden and popped them into my carry-on bag.

Customs regulations prevent you from carrying produce into other countries, so my family and I ate the apples on the plane. It comforted me to consume that little touch of home while winging it across the Atlantic to parts unknown.

Even today, whenever I'm traveling, after depositing my luggage in the room, I light a stick of incense and say,

All that's wrong, be gone, be gone!
Life and love come filtering in!

I slowly walk around the perimeter of the room and bathroom, repeating the phrase and letting the sweet fragrance soothe my senses. I even cense the closet. I take a few moments to visualize the room as a safe and restful haven that will allow me to relax and recharge my batteries during a stressful business trip or hectic day of sightseeing.

I then set up an altar cloth from my kit on a table or dresser and light a blue or vanilla-scented candle to foster harmony. Since I adore tea, I always pack tea things, including a proper china cup; my own metal spoon; a selection of herbal, green, and black teas (kept fresh inside a metal pencil box); and my own electric pot. These days, many hotels rooms supply brewing pots, but in my opinion, none of them does as good a job as my own. While I'm waiting for the water to boil, I slip into comfortable sweats, cotton socks, and house slippers, and I pull out a favorite book. Then I sit and unwind

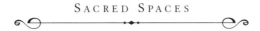

with a cup of tea and have a good read for a half hour or so. Pretty soon I'm feeling so safe and snug, I might almost be in my own home.

SLEEPING OVER

In spite of taking these measures, some people may still feel stressed out in an unfamiliar environment, whether it's a hotel room or the spare bedroom of a friend or relative. My recommendation in these cases is to always perform a protection ritual before retiring. This may be as simple as reciting the Lord's Prayer, performing a meditation, or doing some other series of actions that reflects your spiritual beliefs. When I find myself in new surroundings, I always perform a little ritual from my own spiritual path, which includes reciting, either aloud or silently, the names of the archangels. The process includes some visualization and takes around ten minutes to complete.

TRANSFORMING YOUR OFFICE

Many of us spend more time at work than at home, or at least it seems that way. It can be a daily drudgery to spend all that time commuting and then to sit facing four blank, white walls every day. Worse yet is if you have to cram yourself into a gray cubicle for eight hours or more. It can make the time spent at work crawl at glacial pace.

There are tons of things you can do to turn your work-space into a miniature haven away from home. I'm not prom-ising that your hours in the office will pass like a brief interlude at a symphony. At the same time, a personalized office space might tempt you, like the Seven Dwarves, to "whistle while you work," which will certainly make you happier and more productive. Here's what a colleague of mine has done to turn her office into a home away from home.

Helen the Horsewoman's Office

Helen works for a prestigious intercultural training company, where she receives many clients, resource people, and trainers in her spacious, paneled office. A southwest-facing wall with a glass door opens on a Japanese-style garden and patio. Helen's positioned her desk so she can view the mountains and the cheerful annuals she plants out-side by the door.

In front of the desk, she's positioned two overstuffed easy chairs with a coffee table between them. A crystal vase on the table brims with seasonal candies. Plants drape down from the ceiling, and several others tucked away in corners soften the room's contours. A desk lamp and another lamp on top of a filing cabinet emit a friendly, yellow glow that chases away the harsh glare of the fluorescent lights. On the wall behind the desk under a row of high windows, Helen's strung scores of postcards from happy clients, now residing in eighty countries.

If it weren't for the bank of filing cabinets, the inevitable piles of papers, and the big, dry eraser board announcing the calendar of programs, you'd think you were in someone's living room. Helen has generated this atmosphere to put people at ease and to provide a sanctuary for the other employees in a very busy training center.

She's added personal touches to provide a haven for herself, as well. Her two passions in life—her family and her four horses—are very much in evidence. Pictures of her daughter adorn the desk and filing cabinet, alongside photos of Helen's husband and herself astride their horses. An alpaca llama rug from Peru graces the wall behind the easy chairs, and little figures of horses top the computer and end tables. Two saddle blankets with colorful Southwestern designs serve as throw rugs by the chairs and desk. The mouse pad is a comically grinning portrait of Mr. Ed—Helen thinks that a touch of humor goes a long way toward lightening the workplace environment—and the computer screensaver is a picture of wild horses grazing in a mountain meadow. In these ways, Helen's office offers a private sanctuary and a welcoming parlor rolled into one.

PERSONALIZING YOUR OFFICE CUBICLE

You may not have a large, paneled office like Helen, but you can take advantage of many of the same devices to personalize any area, even one as small as a cubicle. Try adding a table lamp, a cozy-looking throw rug, a couple of postcards, a souvenir from a favorite trip, or an affirmation on top of your computer. A plant or a framed photo go a long way toward making you feel at home in an institutionalized setting.

In fact, did you know that the Germans have a "right to light" law? This innovative piece of legislation proclaims that anybody who works in an office has the right to see natural daylight through a window. This means that the German businesses and corporations have been obliged to transform their offices by tearing down inner walls, rearranging space, and building interior glass doors and windows so that even the most subordinate employee sitting in a cubicle in the center of a room can see some of the world outside.

One day, perhaps such advanced humanitarian ideas for employee comfort and well-being will filter into corporate America. In the meantime, if your cubbyhole doesn't have a window, don't despair. Take photos or collect postcards of beautiful outdoor spots and create a collage on the wall of your cubicle.

While we're on the topic of photos, in a very unofficial survey of office spaces in my town, I found that most people seem to favor pictures of their pets versus friends and relatives. It's a scientifically proven fact that pets help people feel relaxed and content and that pet owners have lower blood pressure. This may account for this phenomenon. Even if you work in a cubicle, you can go one step better. Put a fishbowl on your desk, and stock it with a couple of fish.

Rather than using the styrofoam cups at the office, you can add another homey touch by keeping a china cup in your desk drawer. Next to it, store packets of your favorite brown sugar, special teabags, premium cocoa, a tin of shortbread, or whatever little treat you like most. Remember one of the five senses is taste, and here is where you can splurge.

Depending on the kind of work you do, you might bring in some headphones and a small collection of CDs. Music can relax, but it is also a good way to energize and perhaps even excite your imagination for the work to be completed. Just make sure that your music doesn't disturb your coworkers' productivity. Remember that they're trying to create their own sacred space.

Several of the people interviewed in this book have mentioned the value of humor in a sacred space. I once knew a fellow who worked in an insurance office and kept a rotating joke wall in his cubicle. On this wall he kept five or six cartoons posted, often having to do with the insurance industry. Each time he found a good one, he'd retire the oldest joke and tack the new one in its place. Fellow workers made a point of stopping by to view the latest offerings. The joke wall helped maintain a light and cheerful tone that lifted morale in the office. Here's a word of advice, though: Keep your decorations within acceptable limits. While your office space is a good place to express your interests and personal tastes, don't hang up a six-foot crucifix or a hundred magazine foldouts of pinup girls. You are working in a professional environment, so your area should look professional and respect the feelings and beliefs of others around you.

HOSPITAL ROOMS

The last twenty years or so have seen something of a renaissance in hospital-room design, as patient comfort and security have been shown to play a significant role in recovery. For example, cheerfully painted birthing rooms and tastefully decorated cancer wards furnished with pretty curtains, rocking chairs, welcoming couches, living plants, and video and DVD players lend a homey feel to the space.

Yet no matter how agreeably the room is decorated, the fact remains that the patient is in a hospital and away from the comfort and security of home base. This why I think it's important to always remember patients by sending cards, flowers, or little gifts like CDs, books, a pretty robe, comfortable slippers—whatever you know pleases them most. Once I brought aromatherapy oil to a cancer patient friend. I poured the contents into a little silver bottle attached to a chain so she could wear it like a necklace. She told me that this was the best gift she received while she was ill, because sniffing the fragrance took away the hospital odors and lifted her spirits. When people are undergoing a lot of stress, little touches help brighten and personalize the space. More important, they strengthen the bond to other people and to the outside world, helping to keep the patients from feeling isolated.

MOBILE SACRED SPACE

Cars, trucks, SUVs, motorcycles, even bicycles—any form of personal transportation—also constitute a space where most of us feel we could use a little extra protection. You've certainly seen lucky dice or St. Christopher's medals hanging from motorists' rearview mirrors. Some people like to affix a statue of Buddha or the Virgin of Guadalupe to the dashboard, while others choose to suspend a small crystal from the rearview mirror because it draws light and produces lovely rainbow patterns. Still others prefer to place an item in their car that reminds them of their ethnic origins. This wide range of decorations might include a shamrock, a kachina doll, or something else that identifies the person, like a miniature soccer ball or a tiny running shoe for athletes.

Affirmations written on paper and glued to the dashboard are also popular.

My husband and I have what you might call an offbeat sense of humor when it comes to cars. I've hung from my mirror a picture of Wile E. Coyote lighting a stick of dynamite, while my husband has a rubber statue affixed to the dashboard, the Pink Panther, facing the windshield with hands clenched over his eyes. We think that it takes a good sense of humor to drive in today's traffic with so many disrespectful drivers on the road. Every time we look at the Pink Panther or Wile E. Coyote, it makes us feel good and puts us in a better mood to deal with the craziness going on around us. It helps us feel that our cars are havens of good humor and tranquility as we sail the rough seas of the road.

All this is pretty typical stuff, and you may have already put something like it in your own vehicle. But have you ever conceived of your car as a vehicle to take you closer to heaven? Some African-Americans do.

The Charmed Chevy

When I was a kid living in Detroit, I heard of a man who converted his old Chevy into something of a mobile billboard—at least, that's what most people thought. The car was encrusted with more than a thousand light bulbs, seashells, bits of shiny mirror, and red reflectors sticking out at odd angles. He glued a toilet to the top of the car and coated it with sequins and silver balls. The mirror shards on the back of the toilet formed a large diamond.

Around the side of the car, this gentleman attached handless clocks and a couple of chrome hubcaps. Across the diameter of the hubcaps and the wheels he painted black lines that formed equal-armed crosses. What most people didn't realize was that this fellow decorated his vehicle in this way to symbolize his soul in motion. In the Voodun religion, these kinds of decorations are representative of the movement of the soul as it journeys through the cosmos to unite with the Creator or All-One.

In this sense, the car represented the owner's very private space, the nucleus of his soul. Two basic Creole-Congo concepts are evident in the embellishment of the Chevy. The first is the *dikenga* sign. The *dikenga* is made from a cross in a circle. The cross symbolizes a crossroads, or a boundary between this world and the world of the spirit, while the circle symbolizes the soul's eternal cosmic orbit between birth, life, death, and rebirth. The diamond and triangle shapes are variants of the same idea. In the Congolese spiritual system, the vertical axis of the cross connects God above with the dead below, while the horizontal axis acts as a boundary between the living and the dead. Each arm of the cross mirrors the progress of the immortal soul on its eternal journey. Anything that interrupts this journey may lead to the destruction of the soul. This is why the Chevy was decorated with so many circular symbols, like clocks, and why the wheels included radiating crosses.

The other concept is called "flash-and-light." This refers to the power of light and movement to keep the spirit whole and moving so that once again, it avoids misadventure and destruction. Flash-and-light can also propel the soul on its journey to glory and attract wealth, both on the material and spiritual planes. The symbols used to express this idea on the Chevy included shiny materials, such as light bulbs, tinfoil, bits of broken mirror, chrome hubcaps, sequins, and polished dimes and quarters.

The toilet on top of the car is symbolic of honor and enthronement of the soul. In the days of slavery, African-Americans were accustomed to taking bits and pieces of things that others would discard. They then imbued them with symbolic meaning.

In Chapter 10, we will discuss the ways that the African concepts of *dikenga* and flash-and-light can be applied to permanent sacred spaces, like the home and yard.

NEW BEGINNINGS

In this section, we address the ultimate "home away from home." If you consider your entire home as a sacred place, what happens to it when you change residence? The world is getting to be a smaller place, and many people now hold jobs that will require them at one time or another to live abroad. How do you maintain a sacred space when you move to another country?

Although the prospect of living in a different, possibly exotic location, is exciting, uprooting the family and setting it down in a place where even the most mundane activities, like using the telephone or buying bread, are totally different, can be a daunting experience. Living day-in and day-out in an environment where you're expected to act with normal speed and efficiency, without knowing the rules of the game, can lead to severe intercultural stress. Behavioral psychologists call this culture shock.

One of the antidotes to the stresses of adjusting to life in another culture is to create a home haven as soon as possible. This doesn't mean you should attempt to replicate your family's former physical environment in every detail; that would just put you out-of-step with the new cultural environment. Let me give you an example.

When I lived in Wales, I met another American family in a nearby village. When they moved to Wales, the wife insisted on bringing everything from home, and I mean everything, including potholders and dishtowels. It was as if she suspected the Welsh didn't know how to use them. I, on the other hand, went out and bought tea towels and potholders covered with Welsh vocabulary words accompanied by explanatory pictures.

That way, I easily learned colors, how to count to ten, and the meaning of some geographical terms, like the words for hill, river, and waterfall.

The other American family lived near a U.S. Army base and had friends purchase American products for them from the store on base. I particularly remember the wife showing off cans of American brand soups and gigantic boxes of cereal. The problem was that cupboard shelves in most Welsh houses are shorter and smaller than those in the United States, so they had to store their booty on the kitchen floor. Besides that inconvenience, they ended up missing out on tasting many of the delicious regional products. Needless to say, these people had such an unhappy experience they left before the term of their assignment was over.

To make a haven abroad, I recommend that you take along some familiar things: your son's favorite teddy bear, your daughter's precious rock collection, your husband's beloved spy novels, your own cozy comforter. Familiar home touches that evoke fond remembrances will stand you in good stead when you're feeling lonely, confused, or homesick. At the same time, don't take anything you would feel very sad to lose. For instance, don't take the antique family Bible.

Before you depart, make it a family project to collect and mount photographs in an album. Include pictures of family, friends, pets, home, place of worship, community center, and local landscapes. Albums perform double duty. You can thumb through the photos when you're feeling blue, and you can show them to friends in the new culture when you tell them where you come from.

Before you leave, make sure you also buy a glossy picture book that depicts your place of origin. Since I'm from the Rocky Mountain West, I've taken along books that show the beauties of the high country; tales of the Old West; Native American traditions; Denver, "the Mile-High City"; and homesteaders' quilts. You never know when members of your family may be called on to talk about your home region at a ladies' social, a rotary club–type meeting, or a show-and-tell session at school. Before you return to the States, give the book to a friend's child as a memento.

Another idea to facilitate the adaptation process is to incorporate something from the host environment into your new home. When I moved to Rio, I quickly learned an amazing fact: Plants grow more quickly in the tropics. If I took a cutting from a planter on the sidewalk and stuck it into an empty yogurt cup filled with water, the cutting miraculously took root overnight. I didn't have much furniture when I lived in Rio, but I sure had an apartment full of flourishing greenery.

I also acquired a bird—a turquoise parakeet, to be precise. Since I was in Rio to work on my dissertation, I named him Euclides, after my nineteenth-century author. I loved having a bird. They are popular choices for pets among Brazilians, and this gave me some "conversational currency" to exchange with my friends and neighbors. Since I've moved back home to a houseful of cats, I obviously can't have a bird. However, if you introduce portable things from your new culture, like my Welsh potholders and tea towels, you'll be able to take them home as a fond memory of your stay abroad.

THE CULTURAL ATTACHÉ'S LIVING WALL

I'll never forget the time I visited the U.S. cultural attaché's apartment in Brasilia, the capital of Brazil. The apartment was nice and roomy, if unremarkable, with the exception of the dining area. This room obviously was the woman's sacred space.

She was a gregarious type and enjoyed entertaining. She'd painted the walls a warm mustard color to mimic the tropical sunshine. Potted palms, pineapples, and some kind of ivy cascaded from the corners. Just outside the French doors on the veranda, the attaché had set up a small mechanical waterfall, and the water tinkled melodiously in the background. A magnificent, Portuguese Colonial–style table and six chairs dominated the center of the room. The matching sideboard was the only other article of furniture.

All this formed a backdrop to the real center of attraction, which consisted of a long expanse of wall covered from ceiling to floor with primitive paintings bursting with color. My friend explained that whenever she traveled, she made a point to visit local craft fairs where artisans gathered every Sunday to set up booths. She always chose pictures that depicted some aspect of Brazilian country or domestic life: rubber collectors in the Amazon; white-clad, turbaned women dancing at a festival in the northeast; coffee pickers in the fields of the south; and vendors hawking homage treats, that is, sweets associated with the gods of the Afro-Brazilian pantheon, at the beach. The quality of the artwork varied, and some of it was quite good. What mattered most was that she had assembled a vibrant, breathing tribute to Brazil's cultural heritage. She could return home with her "living wall" and reassemble it as an elegant and significant personal memory of her time abroad.

Even if you're planning a domestic move, you can help smooth the transition by adapting many of the abovementioned tips to fit your individual circumstances.

Chapter 10

Sacred Space As an Expression
of Cultural Identity

We ended Chapter 9 with a discussion of what people do to create a sacred space when living abroad. Now, let's steer the conversation toward the topic of sacred space as an expression of cultural identity. Back in Chapter 1, we discussed the ways a personal space both includes and excludes the outside world by identifying differences and recombining them synergistically.

In this chapter, I describe some unique ways in which people from cultures worldwide have made personal spaces. You don't have to be a follower of any of the traditions presented in this chapter. Let the stories inspire you to incorporate some of the innovative solutions into your own sacred space.

RUSSIAN "BEAUTIFUL CORNERS"

Krasny ugol, which translates from the Russian as "beautiful corner," refers to the corner of a room where Russians traditionally keep their sacred images and pictures of saints. The icons are hung on the wall or placed on a beautifully carved shelf or cabinet made from birch wood, pine, or fir. If the householders are artsy, they may embellish the shelf with handsome renditions of birds, herbs, or flowers indigenous to their native land. They may also cover the shelf with a hand-embroidered cloth or sew a curtain to frame the icons. A lighted candle or a small hanging lamp illuminates the pictures. Honored guests are seated in this corner by the altar, which often faces a massive, masonry stove built in the opposite corner that radiates warmth and hospitality.

Although you can find "beautiful corners" in many Russian households, they are most often associated with the *izba,* a traditional, almost extinct, type of cottage that is found mainly in the northern provinces. You could think of *izbas* as very large icons, or entire sacred spaces, because they express many longstanding and deeply felt Russian values, such as a deep connection with nature and nostalgia for the simple, rural life. These cabins, which were built from logs hewn from dense forest trees, represent havens in the wild. In former times, the frozen, impenetrable forests were feared because they harbored wolves, bears, and evil spirits. The *izba*

represented a point of light, warmth, comfort, and protection from the alien world.

When country folk built these structures, they took advantage of the colors, textures, and elements of their surroundings by using wood such as grainy silver fir, knotty yellow pine, and smooth, light-colored aspen, which were native to the Russian forest. On the gabled roofs, they carved images of protective sprits and solar discs to confer good fortune on the household. Beams were nailed together with wooden pegs to make the homes easy to disassemble and reconstruct on another site. In this sense, the *izba* constituted a portable haven.

Inside the cabin, beams were left exposed, and built-in wood furniture provided efficient furnishings and showed off the brilliant craftsmanship of the wood construction. Shining painted utensils, toys, pottery, primitive artwork, and pictures from popular magazines adorned the walls and shelves. Shelves, chairs, and beds were brightened with embroidery, intricately worked in geometrical patterns or with designs of flowers, herbs, and domestic and fantastic animals. These designs were rendered in the traditional red and white colors and embroidered into coverings made for everyday use. They were also embroidered in white-on-white for items reserved for special occasions. In the wintertime, instead of lacy curtains, fragrant pine boughs, and colorful berries framed the windows. Dried herbs suspended from the rafters added to the delicious fragrance of the room. Color, texture, fragrance, and the sound of the crackling fire combined to make the *izba* a quintessential feast for the senses.

These days, most *izbas* have disappeared, but the tradition lives on in the gable-roofed, brilliantly painted country homes and fences, and the gravestone markers patterned after the *izbas* and mounted on posts in rural areas. In this way, the Russian people have adapted the country cottage *izba* style to their modern, urban lives.

MEXICAN *OFRENDAS*

On the other side of the globe, Mexican Catholics celebrate November 2, the Day of the Dead, by assembling *ofrendas,* or special altars at gravesides or in homes. This is one way they celebrate the life of a loved one who has passed on or petition the saints for aid and protection. Some altars are small enough to fit into the palm of the hand, while others cover an entire grave. I've even seen altars built in the form of child-size chairs with skulls for legs and feathers forming the backs.

People let their imaginations run wild devising these altars. Traditionally, the structures include red and orange marigolds, a holdover from Aztec times when the flowers honored ancestors. Another customary decoration is colorful banners cut from tissue paper that, at first glance, look like chains

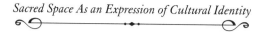
of paper dolls. On closer scrutiny, it becomes apparent that the cutout patterns are not paper dolls, but images of death, such as skulls and skeletons. Sometime before the festival date, a family member might begin crafting the altar by covering a preexisting shelf in the home. The shelf might also be one that the family member actually builds just for the occasion and attaches to a wall in the living room. This shelf serves as the base for the altar and is covered with a gaily-colored oilcloth cut to fit its dimensions, or alternatively, a multicolored miniature serape blanket. A framed photograph of the honored relative is set in a prominent position on the shelf and is lighted by a votive candle in colored glass.

Over time, relatives and friends add mementos, like clay images of objects that were special to the deceased, such as a favorite car, or dollhouse-size books to represent an interest in literature. Miniature plaster platefuls of food that the relative enjoyed are deposited on the shelf, like huevos rancheros, tacos, or enchiladas in brown *mole* sauce, looking so delectable you'd think the food was real. All manner of items might round out the tableau, including feathers, stars, tassels, glitter, little tequila bottles, cigarettes and matchboxes, painted suns, and perhaps even a papier mâché *alebrije,* a figure of a fantastical, bug-eyed, long-tailed, protective creature with sharp teeth. By the time the date arrives, the shelf has been transformed into a glittering memorial to be carried to the cemetery.

If the purpose of the altar is to request spiritual assistance, the petitioner might position a wooden cross on the shelf centered between two votive candles and adorn it with *milagros,* which translates as "miracles." These *milagros* are tiny tin amulets that are used as tangible symbols of what the petitioner is requesting aid for. For example, a sacred heart *milagro* might represent prayers to heal a broken heart, while *milagros* shaped as hands, feet, or other body parts would stand for an area of the human body that has been injured or is diseased. Tiny angels might indicate a wish for divine intercession, while birds might symbolize the return of happiness. When I visited Mexican artist Frieda Kahlo's house in Mexico City, I noticed that one wall of her stairwell was teeming with *milagros,* many of them having to do with pregnancy and childbirth. It had been one of Kahlo's cherished desires to have a baby.

The petitioner might also include a "virtuous horseshoe." These miniature horseshoes are wrapped in colorful satin ribbons and embellished with sequins, tin flowers, glitter, and tinsel. In the center, the petitioner glues a miniature, color picture of a saint, often St. George, the patron saint of protection.

Mexican *ofrendas* have captivated people all over the world. In 1972, the Galería de la Raza in the Mission District of San Francisco mounted an *ofrenda* exhibit for the Day of the Dead. People from many different cultures were so taken with the exhibit and by their own need to honor lost loved ones that

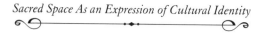
they persuaded the curator to make the exhibit mobile. On November 2, the exhibit and visitors paraded to nearby Garfield Park. The celebrants attached marigolds and written messages for deceased loved ones on the display, as well as food offerings, tin frames with photos of the deceased, and miniature skeletons and skulls. The *ofrenda* parade has become a yearly event, now accompanied by traditional Aztec purification rites and folk dancing.

TURKMAN WEAVINGS

What if the place you lived didn't allow for the luxury of a personal haven? What if you never stayed in one location long enough to establish rapport with a particular place? What if you were a nomad? What would you do?

For centuries, women of the Turkman culture, a nomadic tribe of Central Asia, have used their expertise at weaving to express their individuality. From early childhood, girls learn to weave and embroider everything from towels, pillows, and other household items to prayer rugs and gorgeous flat-woven rugs called *kilims,* which they use to cover the floors of their tents.

Weaving is also a sociable occupation, and women perform it together outside in village squares or inside when visiting each other's homes. They learn to weave patterns and symbols to express personal sentiments, like the longing for a husband, pride in birthing a son, agony over the loss of a child, or contentment in a long-lasting friendship. Thus, their weavings tell a story and reflect the personal expression of the individual weaver.

Symbols, like birds, wild animals, or even geometrical designs, may indicate family or clan associations. The *kilim* or other woven textile becomes a page in the individual's life, a statement to the world about the weaver's relationships, hopes, disappointments, and accomplishments. The woman knows this artifact will last throughout her lifetime, and perhaps for generations beyond as a testament to her cultural identity.

JAPANESE RETREATS

Another country where private space has always been in short supply is Japan. Historically, families have been crowded together in small houses where the walls, which at one time were made from boards and rice paper, abutted their neighbor's equally paper-thin walls. Even today, when many people live in concrete apartment buildings, space is still limited in Japan's highly populous society.

For that reason, the Japanese have devised various ways to honor each other's privacy. Avoiding eye contact, for instance, is a signal that a person wants to be left alone. Meditation is

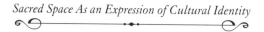

also greatly respected, and people are accustomed to practicing it in the bath or while taking walks in nature. Meditation is also used to withdraw and create inner peace and gain what we in the West would understand as a modicum of privacy. In the past, wealthy householders with enough room for a garden erected teahouses as meditation retreats. Looking out from the teahouse, the contemplator saw a simple but elegant view that changed with the seasons, such as cherry blossoms in the springtime or an intricate pattern of windblown snow in the winter.

Today, few Japanese homes have room for a teahouse. Yet no matter how humble the abode, there is always room for a special place called a *tokonoma*. It consists of a low platform in the main room, where the home's treasure is kept. The treasure is usually something simple, and often ancient, like a scroll on which a beautiful poem or saying is written. To honor it, the homemaker leaves a fresh flower arrangement on the *tokonoma* daily. In this way, a family's cherished heritage is passed from generation to generation.

AFRICAN-AMERICAN YARD SHOWS

In Chapter 9, I introduced you to the African beliefs of *dikenga* and flash-and-light, which are still honored by many black Americans today. I showed how symbols of these concepts have embellished automobiles. These same ideas sometimes find expression in the way the yard and outside of the house are decorated.

The concept of the *dikenga* wheel is often applied to the yard—with one half representing the realm of the living and the other half representing the cemetery, or realm of the dead. Concrete reminders of the householder's ancestors are often displayed in features such as a rock pile in the garden. A tree altar with a meditation chair, a remnant of the times when slaves were only able to worship at trees, may be established in a quiet nook. Protection symbols, such as white-painted tires, mirror shards, or empty baskets placed near the doorway symbolize ways of containing negative energy that might be brought by evil spirits or unwanted visitors. Modern symbols of mobility, such as hubcaps, wheels, miniature airplanes, and bicycle parts, may also festoon a fence as emblems of the soul's journey to glory.

Another protection symbol that is frequently used is called a bottle tree. A dead or living tree is covered with colored glass bottles or plastic bottles filled with colored water. The bottles represent containment of negative energy and thus, in effect, become a means of guarding the threshold. The colored glass also catches the light, replicating the flash-and-light that propels souls to heaven. The concept of flash-and-light, as you recall from Chapter 9, refers to the power of light and movement to keep the spirit whole and moving so that it avoids misadventure and destruction.

The arrangement of the bottles on the tree is purposefully asymmetrical, as are other items that are seemingly strewn at random around the yard. This kind of positioning, which can be compared to the concept of syncopation in jazz, is orchestrated to produce astonishment and also to show a sense of humor. As with all of these mystical symbols of the faith, a double-edged meaning is apparent. On one side, the householder is saying, "The cemetery and the yard are a single unit. Behold the dead, who are watching over this home. If you come with the intent to harm us, you will find a dead tree, a dead branch and broken glass. May you join the dead in the cemetery! But if you approach us in good faith, your soul will be strengthened by the power of the light."

By erecting a yard show, the dweller constructs a sacred space that protects the home, facilitates the journey of the soul, and also expresses a unique cultural heritage to the world. So the next time you see a pile of junk in someone's yard, take a second look. It may be a yard show full of deeply symbolic meaning.

Chapter 11

Sacred Sites Around the World

n Chapter 10, we explored ways in which people world-wide have constructed sacred spaces to express their cultural identity. In this final chapter, I'd like to discuss sacred sites around the world and describe a few of my personal favorites.

The concept of a group of revered sacred sites is not new. A list of the seven wonders of the ancient world was drawn up long ago, during the Middle Ages. The list consists of constructions built between 3000 B.C. and A.D. 476. The seven wonders of the ancient world were remarkable because they reflected the ability of humans to exert their control over nature by making changes in the landscape. The seven wonders were gigantic, but elegant, structures that celebrated religious beliefs, mythology, and the artistic expression of ancient peoples who created them. They have also withstood the ravages of time and the shifting tides of history and politics and thus have become an enduring legacy for mankind. The list includes these sites:

1. The Great Pyramid of Giza, a gigantic stone tomb constructed for an Egyptian pharaoh, located near the ancient city of Memphis

2. The Hanging Gardens of Babylon, a legendary palace with magnificent gardens built along the banks of the Euphrates River

3. The Statue at Olympia of Zeus, the father of the Greek gods

4. The Temple of Artemis at Ephesus in Asia Minor, created to honor another Greek deity, the goddess of the forest and the hunt

5. The Mausoleum of Halicarnassus, another tomb, this one erected for a Persian king

6. The Colossus of Rhodes, yet another Greek statue, carved in the image of Helios, the sun-god, which was erected over the harbor of the Mediterranean island of Rhodes

7. The Lighthouse at Alexandria, a monument built by the Ptolemies on the island of Pharos

CONTEMPORARY TOP TEN DESTINATIONS

Today, the concept of what constitutes a world wonder has changed somewhat, and we now include many natural phenomena as well as those fabricated by humankind. Millions of people undertake long, and sometimes difficult, journeys to visit these locations every year in very much the same way they did in times gone by. The pyramid at Giza has endured until the present day, and still heads the list of top ten travel destinations. It is followed by these wonders of man and nature:

- The Grand Canyon, in Arizona
- The Great Wall of China
- The Taj Mahal, in India
- The Serengeti migration, in Africa
- Machu Picchu, in Peru
- The Roman Coliseum, in Italy
- The continent of Antarctica
- The Amazon rain forest, in South America
- The Iguaçu Falls, also in South America

My short list of four personal favorites, described below, includes one of these worldwide favorite locations.

IGUAÇU FALLS

If the people of the ancient world had known of the existence of the Iguaçu Falls, they surely would have named it among the wonders of the world. The falls are reached by journeying deep into the interior of the South American continent to the area where Brazil, Argentina, and Paraguay share a border. If you've ever seen the movie *The Mission,* starring Jeremy Irons, you will remember the falls, because many scenes were filmed there.

The Iguaçu Falls ranks as one of my favorite sites even though no cultures have designated it as an official sacred location. In the modern era, many people have made the pilgrimage to the spot to observe, feel, hear, smell, and perhaps even taste the unparalleled power of nature as water rushes to meet the earth. The Guaraní Indians named the place Iguaçu, meaning "great water," and this is no understatement. The largest and widest group of waterfalls in the world, 275 individual cascades extend along a crescent-shaped rim for approximately 2.5 miles. The water here plunges 269 feet into the Iguaçu River at the average rate of 1.2 million cubic meters per second.

The cascade called A Garganta do Diabo ("the devil's throat") arguably offers the most dramatic views. This 297-foot waterfall, the height of a twenty-four-story building, is formed in the shape of an elongated horseshoe. It is reached by trekking through semideciduous and tropical woods bursting with richly varied flora and fauna. Pines, palms, and bamboos rub shoulders, while lush mosses, trailing vines, and colorful orchids and begonias abound as far as the eye can see. When you arrive at the waterfall, the awe-inspiring view and thunderous roar take your breath away. Instantly you understand how this waterfall received its name.

It is impossible not to be profoundly moved by such magnificent scenery. For that reason, and also because the place so dramatically manifests the raw powers of the elements, I count Iguaçu Falls among my cherished sacred sites. Evidently UNESCO (United Nations Educational, Scientific, and Cultural Organization) feels much the same way; in 1986, it declared the falls a Natural Heritage of Mankind.

AVEBURY

Folks in ancient times were more attuned to nature than we are in our lives today, and they established millions of sacred sites worldwide. These early people felt that the forces of nature vibrated most strongly in certain places. They built their so-called "houses of worship," or shrines, in these spots as a way to honor nature and the gods they created to represent these powers. Often the sacred sites were constructed in the form of stone circles. Nowhere are these circles more evident than in the United Kingdom, where literally thousands still exist. Many readers undoubtedly have heard of the world-renowned Stonehenge circle, located on the Salisbury Plain in Wiltshire, England. But in the opinion of many, Avebury is more noteworthy.

Avebury is named for the village that lies within these three prehistoric stone circles. The circles cover twenty-eight acres and are bounded by a deep ditch. Over time, several segments of the circles have disappeared, usually because stones were used to construct buildings in the village. Nevertheless, enough of the original structure remains to show that Avebury evidently was an extraordinary sacred space in constant use from the Neolithic to the Bronze Age.

The remains of two avenues lined with standing stones present a striking feature of this construction. One avenue leads 1½ miles from Avebury toward a small stone circle, while the other goes toward another town. The fact that the avenues are laid out in an undulating pattern has led some researchers to posit that the avenues mimic the movements of snakes, and that a cult or cults revolving around serpent worship were active there in prehistoric times. Serpents were once believed to increase fertility in humans, to restore youth, and to confer immortality on their worshippers. So it is possible that the avenues were used as venues for some sort of fertility rituals.

Other indications support the fertility rite theory. Along the avenues, tall, narrow standing stones representative of phalluses alternate with squat, flat, diamond-shaped stones that symbolize the female principle. "Male" and "female" stones face each other across the avenues, almost as if they were lining up to perform a mating dance.

The reason Avebury makes my short list is due to the energy I felt when I visited the stones. Eminent dowsers, like Paul Devereux and Tom Graves, have experienced the same sensation. A dowser is a person who uses a forked stick to find well water and buried treasure. Several of these sensitive investigators have felt a tingling sensation like an electrical charge pass through their hands and arms when they touched the stones. At the same time, they also received the impression that the rocks moved, even though they knew the stones did not shift position in a physical way.

As in feng shui, which uses shapes to direct the flow of chí, dowsers believe that stones of different shapes can both retain and emit energy. Perhaps what the dowsers and I have experienced when we touched these stones is two thousand years of contained sexual energy that human beings stored in them eons ago. Because I am profoundly moved by the possibility of having made a connection with people from so far in the past, I include Avebury in my list.

CLIFF DWELLINGS OF MESA VERDE

Another of my sacred sites centers upon stones as well, but these stones have been used in ways other than to construct circles and avenues. I'm referring to the cliff dwellings that were built by the Anasazi Indians, who lived on what is now a Ute Indian reservation in the Four Corners area of southwest Colorado. More than 4,000 sites in this area are now under the protection of Mesa Verde National Park.

Instead of religious sites, most of the elaborate stone structures constructed in the recesses of canyon walls were designed as homes and storage units. They were built between A.D. 1200 and 1300. The choice of location is puzzling because more appropriate terrain that had previously been settled existed nearby. The community was abandoned just as quickly and mysteriously as it had been built. It has been proposed that the Anasazi were either driven out by invaders or, more probably, that they left the region under the specter of drought.

The dwellings are extraordinary for many reasons. The houses are strung out higgledy-piggledy around the cliff, ranging in size from a single cubicle to the Cliff Palace that boasts 217 rooms. The builders fitted the dwellings into natural alcoves that protected them from the ravages of weather and erosion, so they have miraculously stayed in relatively good shape. In fact, when you view the dwellings from afar, you might think that the community still teems with residents.

The masonry work varies from rough sandstone construction to well-shaped stones. Many rooms are plastered on the inside and decorated with painted designs. From the artifacts found around the sites, it is obvious that the Anasazi were accomplished at using stone, wood, and copper tools, and were expert pottery and basketry craftsmen. This was, indeed, an advanced civilization.

What attracts me to the location is its eerie ambience. When I explore these dwellings located below a high, dry plateau and surrounded by piñon trees, juniper, and sagebrush, I see a testament to a high culture that made a lasting impression on the landscape over a very short period of time. I am entranced by the mystery of these people. I wonder who they were, why they built the dwellings in the first place, and what strange forces made them suddenly vanish. I am also overcome by a certain sense of sadness and nostalgia for a way of life long extinct that never will return to this earth. As with Avebury, the connection with the people is what draws me to Mesa Verde.

SANTIAGO DE COMPOSTELA

The number-one position on my list, however, has to go to the Spanish city of Santiago de Compostela and its cathedral. This town was built during medieval times in the northwest corner of Spain in the region of Galicia. It has recently become famous because Shirley Maclaine wrote a book about a pilgrimage she undertook along the Santiago de Compostela Trail, which extends 500 miles from the French border to the Cathedral of St. James the Apostle in Santiago.

I visited the city a few years ago, and in my opinion, the entire town of Santiago de Compostela should rank as a sacred site. It is truly a miraculous city. Back in the ninth century, the tomb of the apostle James was discovered here, on the site of an ancient Celtic hill fort and Roman town. Alfonso II El Casto heard about this miracle and ordered that a small church be built on the hill. The original structure was destroyed, but the tomb remained intact. A cathedral was erected over the ruins in the eleventh century. During the Middle Ages, the Church offered plenary indulgences and remissions of sins to pilgrims who journeyed along the trail to the cathedral and the tomb. Millions of pilgrims have been streaming to this destination ever since.

One of the first things to notice about Santiago de Compostela is that almost every kind of architecture is represented, from simple Romanesque arches to baroque and Plateresque doorways and windows with their exuberant scrolls and filigreed designs carved from noble gray stone. The rich, green, rugged landscape rivals the verdure of Ireland, and the rain covers the picturesque, old buildings with a soft iridescence that is best enjoyed when strolling around at night in the company of a loved one.

The narrow streets wend their way uphill, eventually leading to a huge plaza dominated by the Cathedral of St. James the Apostle. The cathedral is a baroque structure of epic proportions. Giant columns support story upon story of grand statues of robed figures. Two magnificent towers stretch toward the heavens. The building reigns over the square like an enduring patriarch, proud to show the world the knowledge, wisdom, and spirituality it holds within its walls. Through the door of the façade is the Portico de la Gloria, also known as "the miracle in stone." Carved from the top half of the middle pillar of the portico is a statue of St. James. It is customary for pilgrims upon arriving at the end of the trail to touch the bare area beneath the statue as acknowledgement that they have completed their journey. So many hands have pressed the pillar that a handprint has been worn into the stone. Touching that human imprint connects me with the generations who have gone before.

Perhaps Santiago's most precious resource is its people. One could say that in spite of its ancient buildings and small size, this town is as cosmopolitan as Paris, Rome, or London. For a thousand years, everyone from kings and bishops to merchants, doctors, prostitutes, cardsharps, and beggars have made the pilgrimage to the cathedral and left their mark. From the Pyrenees to the valleys and plains of northern Spain, princes, mystics, adventurers, and common laborers have worn smooth the 500 miles of ground that make up the Santiago de

Compostela Trail. Some have undertaken the arduous journey to find spiritual enlightenment, while others have sought absolution for their sins or, perhaps, to bring a request that God perform a miracle for them.

In summary, I can only say that Santiago de Compostela tops my list of sacred sites because of its majesty and also because of the soul of the place—the indomitable spirit of humanity seen at its highest level of inspiration.

FINAL THOUGHTS

I've been having so much fun sitting at the computer set up at my kitchen table, downing countless cups of my spicy apple and peppermint tea and visiting with you, that I've hardly realized the passing time. I've talked about the nature of sacred space and how important it is to make sure your place stimulates the five senses. Together, we've explored all kinds of spaces, both permanent and temporary, indoors and outdoors, at home, and around the world.

I've also introduced you to some of my friends and colleagues, and you've taken a peek at their personal havens. They don't always agree on every point, like whether you should create the space all at once or let it develop over time, or whether or not you should use music and scent. But that's just human nature. Their differences go to show how unique private space really is, as well as to illustrate that there are no rights or wrongs in this business.

I hope I've entertained and inspired you with ideas for designing your own special retreat. I thank you for inviting me into your personal space and wish you peace and joy in your haven.

Appendix

This appendix is filled with information designed to help you embellish your sacred space. In this detailed reference, you'll find explanations of color symbolism, the significance of particular numbers, and the traditional meanings associated with various animal totems. I've also summarized the healing properties attributed to various gemstones, fragrances, and plants. My explanations are brief, so you might want to use them as jumping-off points for further research. Use the following tips as inspiration for personalizing your altar or sacred space.

COLOR SYMBOLISM

Each color is believed to hold a particular vibration of energy and thus can be used for healing or to facilitate a particular mood. You can refer to the following meanings when planning to decorate a space or when color-coordinating candles to meditation topics.

White: Spirituality, harmony, wholesomeness, cleanliness, purity, generosity, innocence, hope, truth, peace, cherished aims, enlightenment, guidance

Silver: Communication, the mysteries of the universe, stability, clairvoyance, victory of light over darkness

Gray: Stillness, neutrality, deep contemplation, maturity, wisdom

Red: Life, energy, enthusiasm, strength, good health, intensity, love, passion, virility, willpower, courage, movement

Pink: Spiritual awakening, femininity, romance, friendship, good health, beauty, sociability, diplomacy, harmony, selflessness, morality, success, easing of pain, dissolution of negative conditions

Orange: Intellectual stimulation, revitalization, adaptability, concentration, enthusiasm, change of luck, conviviality

Yellow: Change, creativity, inspiration, mental agility, magnetic attraction, communication, harmony, dispelling of discord

Gold: Good fortune, cosmic power, removal of obstacles, good relationships, camaraderie, understanding

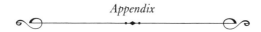

Green: Balance, prosperity, good luck, abundance, success, rejuvenation, equanimity, healing, love, sociability, generosity, fertility, happiness in the home

Blue: Perception, self-knowledge, inspiration, devotion, harmony, serenity, protection, honesty, loyalty, spiritual awareness, guidance, patience, understanding, blessings, joviality, expansiveness

Purple: Spirituality, idealism, deep understanding of the mysteries of the cosmos, spirit communication, power, ambition, overcoming of obstacles

Brown: Neutrality, concentration, intuition, telepathy, bounty of the earth

Black: Deep meditation, protection, receptivity, spirit communication

Note: Black is not actually a color, but the absence of color. Many people associate black with sadness, mourning, and evil and thus feel very uncomfortable having it in their home or their sanctuary. However, black can be used to deflect negativity. Because black holds no color vibration of its own, it can be infused with any vibration of energy. In this sense, black is the ultimate receiver. If black is filled with negativity, it will become bad or destructive. If it is filled with love and beauty, it will shine. One technique you might try is to light black candles in your haven to transform negative experiences into positive ones.

MEANINGS OF GEMSTONES

Healing properties have been ascribed to gemstones for centuries. While some people are skeptical that rocks can exert influences on physical reality, no one disputes their power to bedazzle us. Gemstones can be used in the home to repel certain energies, for aesthetic purposes, or as reminders of qualities to strive for.

Alexandrite: Synthesizes knowledge, strengthens the aura and self-esteem, and inspires creativity and independence of thought

Amber: Protects and creates a friendly, sensual environment

Amethyst: Vibrates compassion, encourages moderation, symbolizes friendship, and clears a troubled mind

Aquamarine: Nurtures harmony in the home, encourages individualism, restores composure after trying incidents, and promotes a blissful love life

Aventurine: Fosters a peaceful environment where inspiration can occur

Carnelian: Suppresses fear, anger, melancholy, and an overactive imagination, and promotes family unity and spiritual upliftment

Chalcedony: Neutralizes negative thoughts, creates an environment conducive to an introspective frame of mind, and improves sour dispositions

Chrysoprase: Calms the nerves and balances the personality, forges links to greenery, growth, and beginnings

Citrine: Counterbalances negative thoughts, stabilizes the emotions, attracts transformative energy, and inspires love of humanity

Coral: Protects, confers wisdom, and enflames sexual attraction

Emerald: Balances the personality, facilitates communication, increases passion, and strengthens resolve

Fluorite: Heals relationships, facilitates concentration, and aids communication

Garnet: Inculcates sentiments of courage, fortitude, and devotion, draws good health, eliminates feelings of fear and guilt, and fires ambition

Jade: Restores tranquility, inspires courage, confers wisdom, and foments self-esteem

Jet: Stands for spiritual strength (which is one of the reasons many rosaries are made from it)

Lapis lazuli: Kindles love and fidelity, strengthens the will, dispels melancholy, aids self-realization, and improves communicative abilities

Malachite: Helps humans decipher the language of animals, cultivates empathy with pets, and promotes a restful night's sleep

Onyx: Hones listening skills, improves concentration, calms fears of the unknown, and promotes renewal

Peridot: Facilitates research and problem solving, symbolizes enjoyment of the modest things in life and innocent pleasures, attracts friends, energizes the body, and allays delusions, fears, and pangs of homesickness

Quartz: Clear quartz crystals probably are the most popular gemstone choice for people wishing to enhance their personal space. Volumes could be, and have been, written about the virtues of this multitalented stone. I can mention only a few of its uses in this appendix. It is a tool to fire the imagination, open the intuitive centers, and heal illness. Early Christians saw in it a symbol of the immaculate conception.

Sapphire: Inspires devotion, spiritual enlightenment, and high aspirations, enables peace of mind, promotes friendships, helps a person achieve independence, and induces clear vision and insight

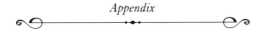

Topaz: Develops leadership, creativity, wisdom, and nobility, builds trust, furthers friendships, and brings happiness

Tourmaline: Creates goodwill, joy, and self-confidence, assists understanding of others, and repels negativity

Turquoise: Protects, helps the possessor withstand melancholy, fosters peace to the home, and enhances understanding of life's truths. The color of this stone is especially conducive to meditation.

SIGNIFICANCE OF NUMBERS

Although you can exhibit any number of items on your altar, some people like to vary their displays according to the season or their mood or intention. For example, you might place one crystal on your altar to symbolize the New Year or when you are trying to create a new beginning. You might light six candles in your sacred space to remind yourself to do six things to help others during a particular time. Here are some traditional meanings for numbers to help you expand on your intentions.

1: The self, independence, strength, beginnings, especially of an enterprise or romance, good luck

2: Union, second chance, change of residence

3: Joy, creativity, new skills, short journeys, friends, relatives

4: Gain, achievement, security, home, real estate

5: Conflict, foreign affairs, legal matters

6: Perfection, creativity, justice, health, pets

7: Good luck, wisdom, the occult

8: Renewal, change in circumstances

9: Wish fulfillment, spirituality, assistance

10: Marriage

11: Change

12: Hiatus, success

13: Transformation

Naturally, many other numbers carry symbolic values. However, I include only thirteen in this list because in my opinion, more than thirteen items clutter an altar.

TOTEMS

Folklore traditions worldwide have attributed particular meaning to various animals. Native Americans, in particular, believe that qualities or "energies" of animals can provide insights for guiding our own actions or behavior. If you have always resonated with a particular animal without knowing why, or if you want to adopt a totem for your sacred space, use the guide below to look up its meaning.

Alligator: Longevity

Ant: Hard work for gain, thrift, good organizational skills, successful partnerships

Bat: Protection, longevity, happiness

Bear: Wisdom, comfort, a safe haven

Bee: Domestic bliss, a busy person, prosperity, public success

Beetle: In ancient Egypt, the beetle, or scarab, was an important symbol of creation, transformation, and renewal. It also stands for fortitude and eternal life.

Bird: The kind of bird dictates the meaning.

Bull: Creativity, fertility, strength, masculinity, decisiveness, the zodiac sign Taurus

Butterfly: Enjoyable pastimes, transformation

Camel: Fortitude, wealth, the Middle East

Cat: Psychic development, independence; if seated, good luck, happiness

Cattle: Prosperity, peace

Chicken: Industriousness

Cock: Financial independence, a confident person

Cow: Beauty, creation, fertility, peace of mind

Coyote: A trickster, entertaining pastimes, an issue that needs study from many viewpoints

Crab: The zodiac sign Cancer, a many-sided issue

Dog: Faithfulness, protection, the Guiding Light; bulldog—tenacity

Dolphin: A well-deserved reward, rescue, recovery from an illness

Donkey: Patience, self-sacrifice, inheritance

Dragon: Great power, sudden change

Duck: Money, fidelity, good luck in speculation

Eagle: Power, fame, change for the better

Fish: Salvation, good fortune, success, fertility, productivity, the zodiac sign Pisces

Frog: Creativity, fertility, pregnancy, abundance, success through changing job or home, transformation

Giraffe: Exotic destinations

Goat: Determination, persistence, courage, the zodiac sign Capricorn

Goose in flight: Success, happy trails

Gull: A survivor

Hare/rabbit: Fertility

Hen: Fertility, domestic bliss

Heron: Intuition, organizational skills

Horse: The zodiac sign Sagittarius, inner strength, a beneficial change, good luck

Kangaroo: Domestic harmony, fast progress, the country Australia

Lion: The zodiac sign Leo, ambition, prosperity, the performing arts

Owl: Truth, wisdom, patience, psychic self-development, a mystery, a night person, spirit contact

Parrot: Love of the tropics

Peacock: Riches, a prosperous estate

Phoenix: Rebirth, longevity, domestic tranquility, peace, prosperity, benevolence, empire, fidelity, justice, obedience, rectitude

Pig: Good fortune, financial success, a happy-go-lucky person, a banker

Raven/crow: A messenger, change in consciousness

Snakes (intertwined): Healing, sexual union, prophecy

Spider: Good luck, self-determination, cunning, intrigue, industrious labor, persistence

Squirrel: Hard work, progress, abundance

Swan: Contentment, mysticism, everlasting love, involvement with music

Tortoise/turtle: Creativity, achievement of aims

Unicorn: Secret relationship, chastity, self-sacrifice, psychic talents

Whale: Resounding success, a maternal figure

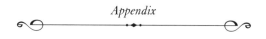

FRAGRANCES

I've written this section with perfume and incense fragrances in mind. Nonetheless, you can obtain similar effects by adding a certain plant to your space because most of the scents outlined below are plant-derived. The term in parentheses gives the main description for the kind of odor associated with the scent. Many scented oils are very concentrated and not produced for human consumption, even if they are edible. My advice is to never consume any perfume or scent oil unless the directions on the bottle specifically direct you to do so.

Basil (herbal): A strengthener; self-regeneration, achievement, mental activity, love

Benzoin (resinous): An antifungal that strengthens the heart chakra; protection, purification, self-confidence, self-growth, peace of mind

Bergamot (citrus): An antidepressant; protection, motivation

Bitter Almond (fruity): A stabilizer; magnetism, love, harmony, prosperity

Cardamom (spicy): A stimulant; love and passion

Chamomile (fruity): A calmative; healing, passion

Cherry (fruity): An astringent; education, spiritual awareness, social adaptability

Cinnamon (spicy): A germicide; purification, blessing, abundance, communication, creativity, sexuality

Civet (animal): Attraction, spiritual guidance

Clove (spicy): An antiseptic; sexuality, protection, energy booster. Not recommended during pregnancy.

Clover (grassy): An alterative; success, faithfulness, protection

Eucalyptus (refreshing): An antiseptic; purification, good health. Do not take internally.

Fir (woodsy): A warming scent; mental clarity and vision, healing

Frankincense (resinous): An anti-inflammatory that opens the chakras to spiritual growth; invocation, protection, success, prosperity, aura cleansing, prayer

Jasmine (flowery): An antidepressant that stimulates the creativity center of the brain; love, sensuality, success

Lavender (refreshing): A normalizer; heightened awareness, grounding and centering, meditation

Melissa (citrus): An antiseptic and sedative; communication, reproduction, past-life recall

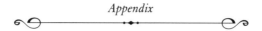

Musk (animal): A chakra opener; love, affection, eroticism, prosperity. Use of a synthetic is recommended so a musk deer doesn't have to die to provide the scent.

Neroli (flowery): A calmative that stimulates the heart chakra; love, sex, good health, peace and harmony, positive, directed energy

Oakmoss (grassy): A fixative; the Earth, love. Do not take internally.

Patchouli (animal): An astringent; love, prosperity, protection, the Earth

Peppermint (refreshing): A decongestant; energy, memory, partnership

Pine (resinous): A stimulator of the adrenal cortex; spiritual upliftment, purification, strength, fortitude, peace of mind

Queen of the Meadow (grassy): An internal body cleanser; healing, meditation, peace, visions of the future

Rose (flowery): A mood elevator that stimulates the heart chakra; love, high aspirations, beauty

Rosemary (herbal): A stimulant and fumigant; self-development, memory, meditations for serenity and wisdom, fountain of youth

Sandalwood (woodsy): A mood elevator; purification, concentration, meditation, past-life recall, grounding, relaxation, openness

Tangerine (citrus): A cleanser; concentrated energy

Thyme (herbal): An antibacterial; memory, upliftment, concentration, family health, astral travel, protection

Vetiver (woodsy): A skin softener that also stimulates the root chakra; success, luck, comfort, grounding

BOTANICALS

It would take volumes to describe all the plants that would make good choices for your indoor or outdoor sanctuary. In the meantime, I've narrowed the selection down to a handful of my favorites. To give you a wide range to work with, I've tried to choose some houseplants, flowers, trees, herbs, as well as a few botanicals you can make teas from or eat. All the following botanicals are edible, but some are used mainly for garnishes. These tend to be bitter and are probably not something you'd enjoy eating. I have made comments on edibility after each entry.

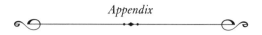

Aloe Vera

This succulent perennial of the lily family is native to the West Indies, where it blooms all year long. It's a popular houseplant in northern climes, and is readily available at florist shops, nurseries, and even the grocery store. Ancient Egyptians considered the aloe plant an emblem of their faith, and they hung it from their doorways as a sign that the dweller had made a religious pilgrimage. In folk tradition, this botanical is associated with love and the strengthening of bonds between people. (Aloe vera is edible, but some varieties are extremely bitter.)

Carnation

Some of the fragrantly scented blooms of this frilly flower hail from the state of Colorado. In general, the red varieties are more heavily perfumed than the yellow or white, but these days it's hard to tell whether a carnation is truly red because of flower spray-painting.

An interesting way to take advantage of the spicy carnation scent at the festive dinner table is to do as the Romans did and float the blossoms in glasses of water, warmed from below by votive candles. According to myth, the religiously inclined are attracted to white carnations, and those who crave to do things in a grandiose manner are drawn to the red variety.

Carnations symbolize femininity, gentle love, allurement, and fidelity. The official flower of Mother's Day, carnations represent motherly love. The flower is also associated with joy, and it is alleged to help preserve the human body and chase away nightmares. (Carnations can be used as a garnish in cooking although some people, including me, don't especially care for the flavor.)

Chamomile

The daisy-like, apple-scented flower of this delicate-looking herb is a delight to behold. When planted near other herbs, chamomile helps them grow. It also attracts beneficial insects to the garden. The herbal, bittersweet apple taste of the flowers is popular in tea as well as an additive in shampoo. Such a versatile plant for your garden haven!

In old times, this herb grew in the pathways of pilgrims, who released its fragrance in the air when they stepped on it. Because of this, it was quipped that "the chamomile shall teach the patience that rises best when trodden upon." Perhaps this is why this herb has come to stand for perseverance in adversity and humility. The essence is alleged to help a person overcome feelings of melancholy and anger. (Chamomile flowers are edible.)

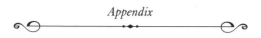

Cranesbill (Geranium)

This is not the popular window-box flower, but a wild plant with pinkish-purplish five-petaled flowers that bloom in clusters at the end of each stem. Native to North America, cranesbill thrives in the woods in the eastern part of the United States. In cooking, it lends an exotic flavor to many dishes. Cranesbill combines well with blackberries, lemon, and ice water and also perks up the scent of rosewater.

Native North Americans once relied on this herb as a method of birth control. According to aromatherapists, a cranesbill decoction reduces yin/yang extremes, calms the nerves, aids the transition through menopause, and is a good antiseptic and mosquito repellant. So scatter a few flowerpots of cranesbill around your patio to drive those pesky bugs away. By tradition, the plant has also been used to call on woodland fairies. (Cranesbill flowers are edible.)

Dandelion

The dandelion is ubiquitous worldwide. In fact, it is so common in gardens that it is almost impossible to eradicate. Both the root and the leaves are used medicinally as an astringent, cholagogue, diuretic, galactogogue, hepatic tonic, sedative, and stomachic; the leaves also have a high vitamin C content.

The tea made from this sunny-looking botanical is alleged to draw prosperity and good luck and to make your dreams come true. It also helps overcome emotional pain, according to aromatherapists.

Dill

A hardy annual with umbrella-like flowers, this herb's name comes from the Old Norse *dilla,* meaning "to lull." The leaf and flower are pungent, smelling like a combination of fennel, parsley, and caraway. This common kitchen garden plant, known as the "pickling herb," is used to flavor breads, cakes, seafood, potatoes, sauerkraut, chicken, and breads.

In the old days it was believed that dill oil on a sugar cube was a panacea for children's complaints. People also ate it to promote weight loss. The seeds boiled in wine are considered an aphrodisiac and brain stimulant. Brides, in times gone by, tucked dill into their wedding bouquets to ensure a happy marriage. (Dill is, of course, edible.)

Hibiscus

More than 300 species of this lovely flowering evergreen shrub are known. The red or orange flower petals enhance potpourri and sweeten tea. A tasty juice is made from the flowers in Mexico. The petals also produce a black dye for shoes, hair, and eyebrows.

In the language of flowers, this plant stands for "delicate beauty" and is associated with love, peace, harmony, and tranquility. (Hibiscus flowers are edible.)

Irish Moss

Irish moss is a type of yellow, green, red, or purple seaweed found on beaches along the North Atlantic coast. The seaweed is used as a filler in many foods. In Ireland, it is called "carrageen" after a coastal village where it grows abundantly. It is an emulsifier in facial and body creams.

Irish moss can be used in the garden instead of grass because it grows equally well in sun or shade, stays green most of the year, and has a close growing habit, so it never needs to be mowed. Place the dried moss under your sanctuary's carpet to attract good luck. (Irish moss is edible.)

Juniper

Cultures worldwide have held juniper in high esteem. For example, the ancient Greeks burned the branches to appease the gods of the underworld and drive away evil spirits. In rural England, it was long believed that burning juniper in the hearth fire protected the home. In the Bible, the bush was said to have sheltered baby Jesus from Herod's army. In times gone by, pregnant women also burned the branches during childbirth to prevent fairies from spiriting away newborns and leaving changelings in their places. (The berries are edible.)

Lady's Mantle

The hooked leaves of this elegant member of the rose family are pleated like a lady's cloak of former times, hence the name of the plant. Clusters of small, yellow-green flowers bloom from July to August.

The Latin name links this botanical to alchemy, which is a tribute to the high esteem in which it once was held. Alchemists have attempted to distill essence of lady's mantle to discover the secret of eternal youth. Teas made from this botanical are said to confer self-control, dignity, and distinction. The leaves, if placed under the pillow, are thought to bring untroubled sleep. (Lady's Mantle is edible.)

Lemon Verbena

An infusion of the leaves from this lemon-scented plant can be used as a wash to clear acne. Preparations made with lemon verbena are said to lessen nausea and dizziness, stimulate the

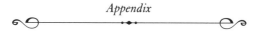

brain, and improve the memory, so it may be tried in postoperative cerebral aneurysm situations or simply to help you acquire better study habits.

In ancient Britain, Druidic women wore garlands of lemon verbena like crowns. Lemon verbena is alleged to attract success to all enterprises and guard against negative thinking. During the sixteenth century, mothers anointed their children with an infusion of the essence because they believed it helped them learn more quickly and gave them a joyous childhood. (Lemon verbena is edible.)

Linden

This stately, deciduous tree attracts myriads of bees to its ambrosial hanging clusters of yellow blossoms in June and July. Linden is said to have a calming effect on the emotions and is drunk as a digestive tonic. Bathe your face in linden flower tea to smooth your skin.

In Greek legend, Zeus traveled across the land of Phrygia and was hospitably received by a faithful old couple. In return, they asked that when it came their time that they might die together. Zeus granted their wish, and at the moment of their deaths, transformed the husband into an oak and the wife into a linden. This is why the tree symbolizes "conjugal love." (Linden is edible.)

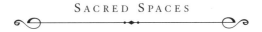
Marigold

The marigold, also known as calendula, is prized for its flowers, which range in color from white to yellow, orange, and deep red. This hardy annual with the aromatic, slightly bitter flowers is easy to grow from seed. The flowers provide an edible garnish and have been used to color everything from cheese and butter to cloth, hair, and soap.

Marigolds are said to encourage visions of the future and help make dreams come true. It is claimed that if you combine essences of marigold, thyme, and meadowsweet and anoint your forehead with the mixture, you will see fairies. By tradition, this flower protects and blesses the departed soul, and encourages merriment. In the Orient, the flower is said to soothe grief. (The flowers are edible.)

Parsley

Parsley is a common biennial kitchen herb of the carrot family. This lacy green herb is frequently used as a garnish. During medieval and Renaissance times, when rivalry and power struggles were common among noble families, parsley was considered an antidote to poisoning. Parsley is also reputed to increase vitality and strength. Perhaps here is one instance of a coincidental relationship between fact and fantasy, as parsley is known to be rich in vitamins A, B1, B2, B3, and C.

The crispy leaves were fashioned into victors' crowns at the Olympic games in ancient times because of their association with strength. Some people still believe that parsley urges on racehorses. Parsley essence is sometimes applied to the skin to facilitate meditation and divination. However, use it with caution as it can cause an allergic reaction in sensitive people, especially when the skin is exposed to direct sunlight. (Parsley is, of course, edible.)

Peppermint

One of the many kinds of hardy, leafy perennial mints that grow throughout the temperate zones, peppermint thrives in damp, shady patches of the garden. Pluto is said to have changed his wife's rival Mentha into a peppermint plant; so this Plutonian herb refers to both the "coldness of fear" and the "warmth of love." The Greeks and Romans crowned their leaders and heroes with peppermint wreaths.

Allegedly, the herb protects against evildoers. The refreshing scent clears the mind, calms the nerves, and is said to encourage prophetic dreams if drunk as a tea before bedtime. It makes a fine ingredient in a sachet to hang in your window altar for good luck, happiness, parting of the ways, new beginnings, transformation, and release of anger. Peppermint, along with ash, basil, periwinkle, sage, and vervain, was used by ancient Celts to purify water for rituals. Be careful when you apply this mint to your skin, as all mint oils can cause irritation. (Peppermint is edible.)

Poppy

Codeine, morphine, and narcotine are extracted from the unripe heads of the strongly narcotic white poppy, but the red variety is perfectly safe to plant in the garden. Poppy seeds from the red variety are widely used in baked goods such as breads, bagels, and muffins for their pleasantly nutty flavor. The seeds also improve the texture of gravies and sauces. Poppies are emblematic of those who have died in war because they flourished in the fields of Flanders, where thousands of troops who lost their lives in World War I are buried. This is why the flower is worn on Veteran's Day. Other traditional associations include empathy, consolation, repose, harmony, peace, psychic dreaming, and fertility. (Poppy seeds are edible.)

Rosemary

The name of this shrubby, tender perennial of the mint family means "sea dew," which refers to the fact that the plant flourishes in poor, dry, calcareous soil near the sea. Sailors can smell its refreshing, resinous odor twenty miles from land. Naturally, the dark-green, needle-like leaves with silver undersides make a pleasant, resinous home air purifier. The

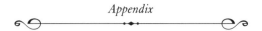

needles exude a crisp aroma when burned as incense. Rose mary is an ingredient of many Celtic incense recipes because it is one of the few incense-making plants that can be grown in Britain.

The herb symbolizes fidelity, for as the age-old saying goes, "Rosemary is for remembrance." It was formerly the custom in Wales for people to remember the dead by carrying garlands of rosemary to funerals and placing them on graves before lowering the coffins into the ground. In ancient Greece, students wore rosemary sprigs in their hair to help them recall their lessons. Thus the plant is associated with knowledge and wisdom.

Rosemary also helps release anger and binds old emotional wounds. Rosemary discourages nightmares, purifies the atmosphere and soothes the troubled spirit, so it makes an excellent plant for your bedroom sanctuary. (Rosemary leaves are edible.)

Sage

This evergreen of the mint family native to the Mediterranean displays grayish-green leaves and blue-violet flowers. Of the many types, the wild variety (*S. sclarea*), native to Colorado, imparts a particularly fresh scent. Many varieties of sage exist, and many plants are called "sage," but not all are related to the salvia. Unrelated plants can be used in incense-making, potpourri, and sachets, but for the most part, they do not substitute well in cooking.

The Latin genus name for sage means "healthy," which should give you some idea of how highly the leaves are regarded in folk medicine.

Aromatherapists claim that if you apply sage or rosemary to your skin, it will regulate the capillary action and revitalize it. Prevent a cold by boiling sage leaves with lemon and honey, and drink the brew. It is said to ease the soreness of tonsillitis. It is also claimed that sage prevents aging and confers wisdom. It is alleged to thrive or wither in the garden according to the fortunes of the property owners. (Sage leaves are edible.)

Violet

The tiny, very fragrant, purple or white flowers of this low-growing plant bloom in April. Some butterflies feed exclusively on their sweet nectar, so you can plant violets to draw these delicate, flighty creatures to your meditation garden. Violets spread easily when planted in grass. The flowers are prized in perfumery and can be crystallized into a sweet violet sugar. The raw flowers also make a pretty edible garnish.

Aromatherapists claim that the fragrance of violets breaks down the barriers of indifference between people and calms strife. The ancient Greeks thought that the calming effects of the scent of violets moderated anger. When Jupiter, out of fear

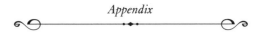

of Juno's jealousy, changed his lover Io into a white heifer, the violet flower sprang from the field and became her food. Because of this legend, violets are now associated with love and healing. Place them in a bowl by a sick person's bed to draw healing vibrations. In folk tradition, it is also believed that to keep a violet plant in the house attracts good luck. (Violets are edible.)

ABOUT THE AUTHOR

Carolina da Silva was raised in Grosse Pointe, Michigan. When she was growing up, she loved taking long walks through her neighborhood and imagining how various homeowners might have decorated their inner sanctums.

She holds a Ph.D. in Luso-Brazilian Studies, has taught literature and language, and currently works as an intercultural trainer and assessor. While living in various countries around the world, she has come to discover and appreciate how and why people from other cultures arrange their sacred spaces.

Among her leisure pursuits are jogging, gardening, herb crafting, tea-making and tealeaf reading, and manufacturing aromatherapy products (which she sells in her mail-order business, Dunraven House).

Carolina makes her home in Boulder, Colorado, where she and her family have enjoyed remodeling their historic home. This sacred space received an award of merit in 2001 from Historic Boulder, and has been featured in a film and a crime fiction novel.